AF328739

THE

LINKEDIN

EDGE

Other books by Jeb Blount

The AI Edge: Sales Strategies for Unleashing the Power of AI to Save Time, Sell More, and Crush the Competition (Wiley, 2024)

Selling in a Crisis: 55 Ways to Stay Motivated and Increase Sales in Volatile Times (Wiley, 2022)

Selling the Price Increase: The Ultimate B2B Field Guide for Raising Prices Without Losing Customers (Wiley, 2022)

Virtual Training: The Art of Conducting Powerful Virtual Training that Engages Learners and Makes Knowledge Stick (Wiley, 2021)

Virtual Selling: A Quick-Start Guide to Leveraging Video, Technology, and Virtual Communication Channels to Engage Remote Buyers and Close Deals Fast (Wiley, 2020)

Inked: The Ultimate Guide to Powerful Closing and Sales Negotiation Tactics that Unlock YES and Seal the Deal (Wiley, 2020)

Fanatical Military Recruiting: The Ultimate Guide to Leveraging High-Impact Prospecting to Engage Qualified Applicants, Win the War for Talent, and Make Mission Fast (Wiley, 2019)

Objections: The Ultimate Guide for Mastering The Art and Science of Getting Past No (Wiley, 2018)

Sales EQ: How Ultra-High Performers Leverage Sales-Specific Emotional Intelligence to Close the Complex Deal (Wiley, 2017)

Fanatical Prospecting: The Ultimate Guide to Opening Sales Conversations and Filling the Pipeline by Leveraging Social Selling, Telephone, E-mail, Text, and Cold Calling (Wiley, 2015)

People Love You: The Real Secret to Delivering Legendary Customer Experiences (Wiley, 2013)

People Follow You: The Real Secret to What Matters Most in Leadership (Wiley, 2011)

People Buy You: The Real Secret to What Matters Most in Business (Wiley, 2010)

NEW SALES STRATEGIES FOR

THE

UNLEASHING THE POWER OF

LINKEDIN

LINKEDIN + AI TO COLD CALL LESS

EDGE

AND SELL MORE

JEB BLOUNT

SALESGRAVY.COM

BRYNNE TILLMAN

WILEY

Library of Congress Cataloging-in-Publication Data is Available:

ISBN: 9781394316717 (Cloth)
ISBN: 9781394316724 (ePub)
ISBN: 9781394316731 (ePDF)

Cover Design and Image: Wiley
Printed and bound by CPI Group (UK) Ltd, Croydon, CR0 4YY
C9781394316717_300925

If you're not on LinkedIn, you simply don't exist in the professional world.

—*Forbes*

CONTENTS

Part 3: Your Network Is Your Net Worth

Part 4: Personal Branding and the LinkedIn Profile Lead Machine

PREFACE

Most sales professionals are desperate to find new techniques to help them break through the noise and get attention, make fewer cold calls, avoid rejection, and have more conversations. Most salespeople want a bigger pipeline filled with qualified opportunities and everyone wants to sell more.

Yet most salespeople overlook or underutilize LinkedIn—the most powerful prospecting tool ever created that, when combined with AI, can give you almost superhuman prospecting powers.

Those who harness the lessons in *The LinkedIn Edge* will transform their prospecting strategy and explode their pipeline with high-quality opportunities. This book is destined to become your essential resource for generating more leads, opening more doors, and engaging in more meaningful conversations.

You should expect nothing less when Jeb Blount, "The Fanatical Prospector," joins forces with Brynne Tillman, "The LinkedIn Whisperer," to teach you exactly how to leverage LinkedIn + AI to cold call less and sell more.

Why LinkedIn, Why Now

It can be argued that the moment that the sales profession changed forever and the door opened to modern selling as we know it was when Alexander Graham Bell said, on the very first telephone call, "Mr. Watson, come here, I want to see you."

The telephone's impact on the sales profession was profound and lasting. Then, as now, the phone remains the most efficient and effective means for conducting real time, synchronous human-to-human conversations with prospects and customers.

Bell made his call to Mr. Watson 150 years ago. Since then only a handful of pivotal technologies have advanced the sales profession with such impact:

- The automobile gave sellers the freedom to cover wider regional territories more efficiently.
- Air travel literally gave sales professionals wings, expanding their reach nationally and globally.
- The internet put unimaginable data at the fingertips of both sales professionals and buyers.
- Smartphones put powerful computers in our pockets and made communication ubiquitous.
- Video calling shrunk the globe and accelerated sales cycles.
- CRM (customer relationship management) made it possible to efficiently capture, organize, and access data.
- Artificial intelligence is transforming the way we develop insight from this data—revolutionizing targeting, outbound prospecting, deal strategy, and forecasting.

But, of all these advances, none has had a more dramatic impact on the sales profession and your ability to connect with almost anybody, anywhere, at any time than LinkedIn.

A Vibrant Sales Ecosystem

LinkedIn is a vibrant ecosystem where a billion business professionals are linked together. Here sales and business opportunities abound. It's a sales Swiss Army knife with dozens of tools and applications for a variety of purposes:

- Prospecting and building pipe
- Networking and referrals
- Research and qualifying
- Multi-threading and stakeholder mapping
- Pre-call planning
- Discovery
- Communicating
- Networking
- Building familiarity
- Personal branding
- Projecting thought leadership and authority
- And so much more

But what makes LinkedIn truly unique is that this giant database and sales ecosystem is constantly self-updating. This means that the data and contacts are never stale. In fact, it is the *only* sales data center where you are always working with the most current information about prospects and their companies.

When you consider that the very essence of selling is connecting with people, building relationships, and solving problems, it's easy to understand why LinkedIn is the most important technological advancement in the history of the sales profession.

This Is a "Fill Up the Pipeline" Book

The LinkedIn Edge is a comprehensive prospecting playbook. You'll gain tools, tactics, and techniques for building a robust pipeline with both short-term and long-game strategies for landing big, lucrative deals and dream accounts.

Prospecting on LinkedIn can feel utterly overwhelming, so we're going to teach you how to:

- Get started.
- Build better prospecting lists and find who and what you are looking for.
- Develop messaging.
- Help people find you and generate inbound leads.
- Communicate and conduct more effective prospecting conversations.
- Generate referrals and warm introductions.
- Reduce resistance and objections.
- Differentiate, build trust, and stand out in a world that wants to commoditize you.

Our mission is to teach you exactly how to enhance, elevate, and accelerate your prospecting efforts by blending LinkedIn seamlessly into your sales tool kit.

We Meet You Where You Are

The problem with most of the books about LinkedIn is that they follow a linear process that doesn't necessarily meet you where you are as a sales professional.

The LinkedIn Edge is different. It is a playbook that makes it easy to dive in right where you need to start, based on your unique situation and immediate priorities. You don't have to read the entire book to get what you need in the moment.

We've sequenced the book into five distinct parts:

Part 1: Fast Prospecting

Part 2: Slow Prospecting

Part 3: Your Network Is Your Net Worth

Part 4: Personal Branding and the LinkedIn Profile
      Lead Machine
Part 5: Differentiation, Thought Leadership, and Authority

Within each part, you'll find the lessons chunked into short, easy-to-consume chapters. Since each aspect of a robust LinkedIn sales strategy is interconnected, you'll find that these lessons build layer by layer to connect the dots. This gives you the flexibility to read the book in either a linear or a nonlinear format.

By engaging fully with the content and exercises provided in this book, you are setting a foundation for leveraging LinkedIn for sustained sales success—to win more, earn more, and sell more. Let's get started.

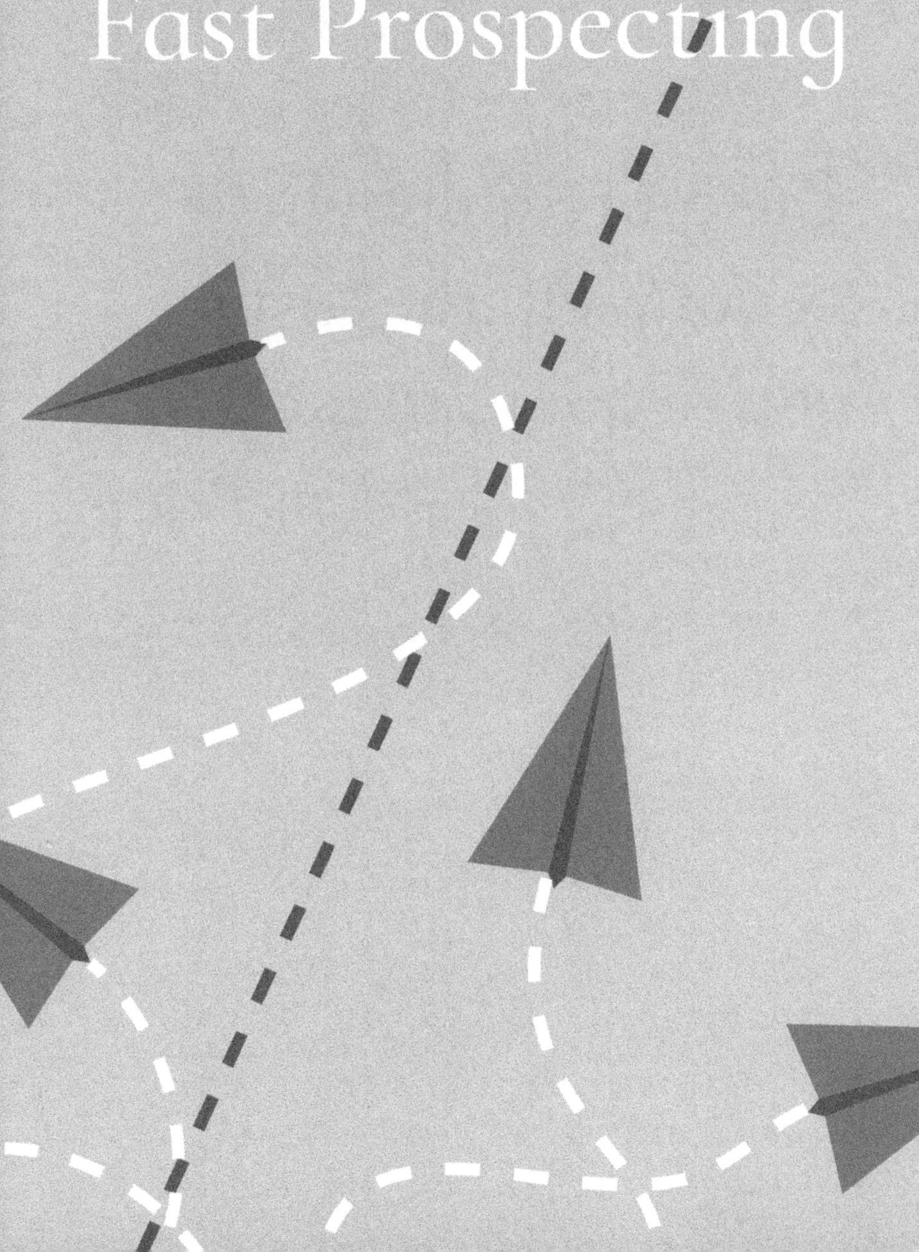

Fast Prospecting

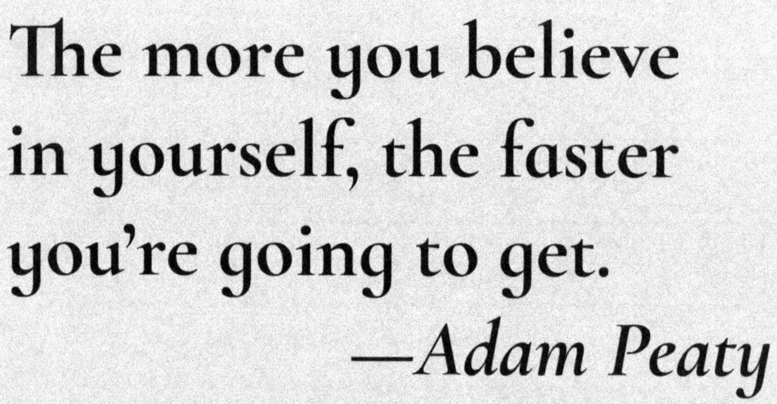

The more you believe in yourself, the faster you're going to get.

—Adam Peaty

1

The Pipe Is Life

Here is a brutal and undeniable truth: The number one reason for failure in sales is an empty pipeline, and the number one reason you have an empty pipeline is that you are not doing enough prospecting.[1]

In sales, everything rests on putting qualified opportunities in your pipeline. Prospecting is the beginning and the end, alpha and omega. It is also the one activity that salespeople despise more than any other.

As a rule, we will do anything in our power to delay, procrastinate, or avoid it. But it doesn't matter how much you hate it; if you don't prospect, you will fail. That is a guaranteed truth.

In modern sales there are two types of prospecting: *fast* and *slow*.

---

[1] See Jeb's book *Fanatical Prospecting: The Ultimate Guide to Opening Sales Conversations and Filling the Pipeline by Leveraging Social Selling, Telephone, Email, Text, and Cold Calling* (Wiley, 2015).

Fast

When you need to build your pipeline *right now*, nothing works better than outbound prospecting. This means taking direct and immediate action to interrupt, engage, and convert leads into qualified pipeline opportunities.

Fast prospecting is rejection-dense, which is why many salespeople shun it. On the other hand, it is incredibly effective for building pipe when done right.

Slow

Slow prospecting is a more nuanced approach. It is still outcome focused—putting qualified opportunities into the pipeline—but here we are playing the long game.

Slow prospecting techniques include inbound lead generation, leveraging your network for warm introductions, nurturing high-value prospects, and cultivating future opportunities. It is relatively rejection-free but requires faith that, by doing the right things consistently, in time you'll get a return on your investment.

Running Fast and Slow

Slow versus fast prospecting isn't a zero-sum game. One isn't better than the other. It's a winning combination.

Embracing this dual prospecting strategy is essential for success in today's noisy marketplace. You must put new opportunities into your pipeline *now* while cultivating future prospects for *later*. Fast prospecting solves the first problem, and slow prospecting the second.

When you're running fast and slow at the same time, you become a prospecting-lead-generating machine, and you can make a lot of money.

Building Pipeline Fast Doesn't Work When You Are Moving Slow

When your pipeline is thin or empty it's like not having enough oxygen to breath. Your highest priority is to fix the problem, *fast*.

Moving fast means interrupting people, engaging them, and converting them into qualified pipeline opportunities. You must dial the phone, knock on doors, send emails, text messages, video messages, and LinkedIn direct messages—even smoke signals if that's what it takes.

When you're a brand-new salesperson starting from square one, because you have no pipe and a short window to ramp up your sales, you cannot rely on LinkedIn alone.

From time to time however, we'll work with new sales reps who will challenge us on this premise. They'll claim that they've learned how to eliminate interrupting people and cold calling with a more powerful LinkedIn strategy that gets results faster.

So we challenge them. They can deploy their slow LinkedIn strategy for a week while Jeb will use a fast prospecting strategy. Here is a synopsis of one of our most recent challenges:

- **New rep:** At the end of the first day, the new rep proudly beamed that his LinkedIn connection requests had been accepted by 16 people and that he'd done a lot of liking, commenting, and sharing. "I made some great connections!"
- **Jeb:** That morning Jeb made 47 dials, had 12 conversations, made one small sale, and set a first-time appointment.

We repeated this exercise for four more days. At the end of the week:

- **New rep:** Added 29 new connections, followed many company pages, posted content, liked content, and conducted lots of research. He'd made *zero* appointments, *zero* sales, added *zero* opportunities to the pipeline.

- **Jeb:** Set eight appointments for initial meetings, closed four more deals, and added three new opportunities to his pipeline.

Jeb used LinkedIn too, but strategically. He built targeted prospect lists, incorporated LinkedIn direct messaging into his multi-channel sequences, and researched prospects to craft more compelling messages. The key difference: Jeb integrated LinkedIn into his complete prospecting system rather than relying on it as his only approach.

The false promise the new rep had bought into was that he could use LinkedIn to build a full pipeline, with minimal effort and no rejection. It doesn't work that way. LinkedIn is not a prospecting panacea. It will not provide an endless stream of inbound leads with little effort.

It is, however, a key component of a complete prospecting system. From list building and direct outreach to lead generation and long-term cultivation of future opportunities, LinkedIn's panorama of features can be a crazy powerful weapon in your prospecting arsenal.

2

Targeting Your ICP

Effective prospecting—fast or slow—begins with targeting the right prospects. Targeting means not random. Randomness is the enemy of effectiveness.

When you need to move fast, spray and pray is a wickedly stupid strategy. Precision will give you a much higher return on your time investment. Therefore, it's essential to have a clear understanding of your Ideal Customer Profile (ICP).

A clearly defined ICP ensures that you are targeting the right prospects and personas (role types), at the right time, with the right message. This clarity significantly enhances your prospecting outcomes.

It's also much easier to craft tailored prospecting messages that connect, engage, and convert when you are focused on a specific ICP.

Go Where the Money Is

When developing your ICP, go where the money is. Your focus is identifying the companies and individuals most likely to buy from you, benefit from your offerings, and become satisfied, profitable, long-term customers.

The starting line for building your ICP is identifying the qualification data points that indicate a prospect is an ideal fit. Here is a list of the qualifiers that you should consider while developing your core ICP qualifiers:

- Industry verticals
- Company size and scale
- Job roles and titles that make and influence buying decisions
- Product, service, and software application
- Geographic location
- Technology stack
- Competitor entrenchment
- Credit worthiness and financial health
- Compelling buying motivations, pain points, and triggers
- Budgetary process and buying windows
- Sales cycle, buying process, and decision timeline

The qualification data points you choose will become your targeting North Star.

Analyze Data Points to Identify Your ICP

Once you've identified your core qualification data points the next step is analyzing the data you've collected. Then use that information to define and hone your ICP. The following exercises will guide you through this process.

EXERCISE 2.1 CURRENT CUSTOMER PATTERNS

Start by analyzing your current customer base. The objective is to find consistent patterns and commonalities among your best customers.

Question	Answer
Which types of customers tend to be most satisfied with your product, software, or service and are most likely to renew, be retained, and purchase more (category, industry, business size, segment, role type, problem solved, use case)?	
List your 10 best/ideal current customers. (Give specific names.)	
What is the title of each decision-maker for these accounts?	

(Continued)

(*Continued*)

Question	Answer
What are the titles of the key decision influencers for each of these accounts?	
What is the industry vertical and size of each account?	
What makes these customers ideal? (Consider revenue, industry, buying process, relationship, growth potential, fit, enjoyable to work with.)	
What problems, challenges, or pain points do you solve for them?	
What made them decide to work with you in the first place?	
What was the trigger event that caused each of these customers to buy from you?	
How have they benefited since working with you? (List the measurable business outcomes you have delivered for them.)	
Describe the common patterns among these top 10 ideal customers.	
What signals on LinkedIn might help you identify similar prospects?	

EXERCISE 2.2 CLOSED WON VERSUS CLOSED LOST

The next step is analyzing the patterns among the deals you are closing versus the ones you are losing. Pull all of your Closed Won and Closed Lost opportunities from the last six months.

Analyze these deals and write down the top 10 commonalities among each type in the comparison table. Look for patterns, including:

- Industry
- Company size (revenue, employee count)
- Geography
- Decision-maker and influencer roles
- Buying triggers (e.g., expansion, compliance changes)
- Pain points
- Sales cycle length
- Objections raised
- Competitors chosen
- Reason for win or loss

Closed Won	Closed Lost
1.	1.
2.	2.
3.	3.
4.	4.
5.	5.
6.	6.
7.	7.
8.	8.
9.	9.
10.	10.

(Continued)

(*Continued*)

Now take a closer look at the Closed Lost column to identify red flags that signal a prospect is a poor fit. Circle these traits or signs so you can avoid them in the future.

EXERCISE 2.3 COMPETITOR ANALYSIS

By analyzing your competitors, you can learn more about their ICP, strengths, weaknesses, and customer segments that you can target and exploit.

Question	Answer
Who is their ideal customer? What patterns emerge in the types of businesses they serve?	
What problems do they claim to solve? Are they addressing different pain points than you?	
What is their core value proposition?	
How do they position their offering? Are they competing on price, service, technology, customization, etc.?	
What are their weaknesses? Where do they struggle, and what customer complaints stand out?	
Where do they win? What types of deals or customers do they seem to attract most?	

Question	Answer
Where do they lose? Are there specific segments where they fail to convert customers or face high churn rates?	
What are the commonalities among customers that they lose to you?	

Consider doing a similar exercise with your competitor's salespeople. Analyze their LinkedIn profiles, messaging, and posts.

AI PRO TIP

Run your competitor's website, LinkedIn team members' profiles, and LinkedIn pages through your AI platform and then prompt your AI to answer the questions in the competitor analysis table. This can greatly speed up the competitor analysis process. Prompt: *"Please analyze [company's LinkedIn page URL] [LinkedIn profile URLs] [website URL] and answer the following questions [list questions] in table format."*

Ask AI to run a SWOT analysis of your competitors and compare it to your own company's SWOT analysis. Ask it to identify your competitive differentiators and gaps. This will help you with positioning your strengths and overcoming objections when prospecting.

Another competitor analysis prompt to consider is this: *"Compare the positives and negatives of these two companies: [company 1] and [company 2] for [your ICP] in [geographic area]."*

EXERCISE 2.4 ICP INSIGHTS

Next, using the information you have gathered, review the ICP insights.

Question	ICP Insights
What industries do your best customers belong to? What company size (revenue, employee count, locations) best fits your solution? Where are these companies located (urban, rural, regional focus)?	
Who are the key decision-makers and influencers? What titles and roles are involved in the buying process? How much influence do they have in making the purchase decision? What are their common professional and emotional motivations for buying from you and your company?	
What challenges do your ideal customers face? What priorities and desired business outcomes drive their decision-making? What problems does your solution help them solve?	

Question	ICP Insights
What trigger event(s) compel(s) potential customers to seek your solution (growth, regulation, leadership changes)? What objections and hard questions do they commonly raise? What is the typical length of their buying cycle?	
What external events indicate that a prospect is ready to buy (mergers, funding, compliance changes)? What technology stack do they use that aligns with your offering? Do they belong to specific associations or attend industry events?	
What types of customers do your competitors target? Where do they succeed, and where do they struggle? How does your value proposition differentiate from theirs?	
Even when a prospect is a fit in every other ICP qualification category, which red flags indicate a poor fit? What stakeholder behaviors suggest a prospect is unlikely to convert?	

Develop Your ICP

Once you've gathered up your insights, you have everything you need to develop your ICP. All you need to do next is synthesize these findings into a clear ICP Blueprint (Table 2.1).

Table 2.1 ICP Blueprint

Qualification Data Point	Your ICP Blueprint
Company Firmographics	*[Industry, revenue range, employee count, geography]*
Decision-Maker Persona	*[Titles, roles, job functions, authority level]*
Pain Points and Challenges	*[Operational inefficiencies, compliance issues, revenue growth struggles, etc.]*
Primary Buying Triggers	*[New funding, mergers, leadership changes, regulatory shifts, market expansion]*
Sales Cycle Expectations	*[Short-term vs. long-term sales cycle, buying committee size, approval processes]*
Technology Stack	*[CRM, ERP, accounting software, marketing automation tools]*
Stakeholder Psychographics	*[Risk-averse vs. risk-tolerant, innovation-driven, service-focused, etc.]*
Disqualification Red Flags	*[Low-revenue, high-churn industry, unwilling to change, misaligned needs]*

Make your ICP as specific as possible. Vague and overgeneralized ICPs will cause your targeting to be scattered and less effective. See the example in Table 2.2.

Table 2.2   Example ICP Blueprint for a Fractional CFO Service Company

Category	ICP Details (Example)
Company Firmographics	Small to mid-sized waste management companies (10–50 trucks), annual revenue of $5M–$50M, located in the southeastern US
Decision-Maker Persona	Owners, CEOs, CFOs, and operations directors responsible for financial and operational strategy
Pain Points and Challenges	Cash flow management, budgeting and forecasting issues, inconsistent financial reporting, struggles with scaling due to poor financial planning
Primary Buying Triggers	Rapid business growth, entering new markets, dealing with regulatory compliance, recent leadership changes, struggling to secure financing
Sales Cycle Expectations	30–90 day sales cycle, decision-making driven by financial pressures or growth initiatives, often requires multiple discussions with owners and advisors
Technology Stack	QuickBooks, Xero, industry-specific ERP systems (e.g., Soft-Pak, Trash Flow), fleet management software, payroll services (ADP, Paychex)
Stakeholder Psychographics	Risk-averse but open to advisory support, highly focused on cost savings and efficiency, prefers industry expertise over generalist financial advisors
Disqualification Factors (Red Flags)	Businesses under $3M revenue, companies without structured bookkeeping, highly resistant to financial guidance, those looking for basic bookkeeping instead of strategic financial support

A Continuous Process of Refinement

The first rule of ICPs is that they are not static. Regularly updating your ICP is crucial. As the economy changes, as your company adds new product categories or moves into new markets you'll need to pivot, expand, and rethink your ICP.

By remaining adaptable and responsive to changes, you ensure that your targeting strategy continues to align with market trends, economic realities, and shifts in your customer base. This continuous process is essential to maintaining ICP clarity and remaining agile in the marketplace.

Coloring Outside the Lines

Effective prospecting activity on LinkedIn—fast or slow—begins with a targeted ICP. The time you invest in refining and applying your ICP pays off in efficiency, better alignment, and a healthier pipeline.

You'll achieve better prospecting outcomes when you make the commitment to stick to your ICP as you build your prospecting lists. Likewise, you'll sell more when you benchmark every prospect, pipeline opportunity, and customer against your ICP and develop the discipline to walk away when they don't fit.

We're not saying that every deal must always fit your ICP perfectly in order to enter your sales pipe. This is not how the real world works. For example, when you need to build your pipeline and generate revenue fast, sometimes you'll need to color outside the lines to find opportunities that you can close right now.

There is a difference, though, between taking a calculated, data-driven risk and chasing a bad deal. If you don't have a clear ICP to guide you, you'll waste a lot of time chasing random prospects that will never become profitable customers.

The end goal is keeping your pipeline full of viable, qualified opportunities that have a high probability of closing and becoming profitable customers.

3

Build Prospecting Lists Fast

Now that you know your ideal customer profile (ICP) you are in position to target the right prospects, at the right time, with the right message. Targeted prospecting lists generate higher response rates and better prospecting outcomes. In this chapter, you'll learn how to leverage five key, non-LinkedIn sources for building winning prospecting lists fast.

Inbound Leads

When you need to build a prospecting list in a hurry, start with the inbound leads that came in over the last past three to six months. These prospects have already expressed some level of interest in what you offer—maybe they downloaded a white paper, attended a webinar, or even reached out directly.

They might have ghosted you or gone quiet, or perhaps you were busy and didn't follow up as aggressively as you should have. Regardless, this is one of the easiest lists to source, and there is a good chance that you can reactivate some of these leads and convert them into pipeline opportunities.

Closed-Lost Deals

Build a list of all of the pipeline opportunities that you lost over the past year plus those of any reps that have left your company. You may need to ask your sales leader for permission to do this, but ask, because it is surprising how much gold you can find in deals that other people have lost.

Because "no decision" is the top reason for losing deals, many of those prospects didn't end up choosing any solution at all—and are still living with the same old problems. They'll likely be open to exploring options.

Research the decision-makers and influencers associated with the closed-lost deals on LinkedIn. You may find that they've left the company, changed roles, or been promoted. This creates opportunities on two fronts.

First, when the original stakeholders move on, especially when no decision was made, it opens the door to restarting the sales process. Go to your prospect's LinkedIn Company Page and identify who took their place. Then send them a personalized connection request.

Second, reach out to the stakeholders who have moved on. There is a very good chance that they are still in the same industry, at companies that have the same problems you solve. Because they are new at their companies, there is a high probability that they will be open to making a change.

Prospects in a Buying Window

Go into your CRM and run a search for prospects that meet your ICP and have an identified buying window in the immediate future. The closer prospects get to a buying window, the more receptive they will be to your outreach.

This buying window could be a contract expiring, a seasonal swing, a budgetary period, equipment coming off lease, or they told you on past prospecting calls to call them back because they would be making changes or decisions at a later date.

Inactive Customers

Inactive or dormant customers are a true gold mine. They've bought from you or your company in the past, but haven't purchased in a while. Or maybe they thought the grass would be greener with your competitor, but are secretly regretting that move.

They are already familiar with your solutions and will be much easier to engage and talk with compared to other prospects. The conversation might be as simple as calling and asking, "When can we expect your next order?" or "What's new on your end since we last worked together?"

Once you've built your inactive customer list, go to LinkedIn and research each contact.

- If they've left their company see the last section for what to do next.

- If they've been promoted, contact them to congratulate and get a warm introduction to the person who took their position and/or research this on LinkedIn.

- If they are still in their position, research their LinkedIn profile and posts to gather information and insights that will help you reengage them in a conversation.

High-Intent Prospects

Intent-based targeting focuses on prospects who match your ICP and indicate that they may be in a buying window based on their online behavior.

AI-powered data platforms, including ZoomInfo and Apollo, track online activity, search behavior, and content consumption from millions of people and companies in real time. Then they use predictive analytics to determine how likely the prospect is to make a buying decision—*the intent threshold.*

Intent data helps you quickly build targeted lists that result in:

- Higher response rates: You're contacting prospects at the right time.
- Shorter sales cycles: They're already considering solutions like yours.
- Better conversion rates: Outreach aligns with real-time interest.

On both of these platforms (among others), you can define your ICP decision-maker roles and set your desired intent threshold. By prioritizing leads based on intent, you'll often shorten the sales cycle and move faster from prospecting to closing.

4

Building Lists from LinkedIn Engagement Signals

Sales is about timing. Get in front of a buyer at the right moment, and the door swings open. Show up too early, and you're ignored. Too late, and they've already signed a deal.

The key to stacking the odds in your favor is building prospecting lists based on real-time buying signals—indicators that someone is ready, or about to be ready, for a conversation.

For example, when a CFO engages with a LinkedIn post about scaling operations, they may be looking for a solution right now. The trick is knowing how to spot these signals, build targeted lists around them, and reach out at the right time—before your competitors do—and strike while the iron is hot.

LinkedIn Post Engagement

When people are posting and engaging on LinkedIn, they are opening a window into their short-term interests, mindsets, and motivations. When someone likes, shares, or comments on a LinkedIn post, they're signaling interest, even if they haven't said a word. Comments also provide a window into the veracity of the prospect's buying motivation.

For this reason, a great source for prospecting list building are the people who have liked, commented, or shared:

- Your posts
- The posts of other people on your team
- Your company page posts
- Competitor employee posts
- Competitor page posts
- Industry expert and thought leader posts
- Industry news posts

Every LinkedIn comment, post like, profile visit, or job change is a digital breadcrumb that opens the opportunity for a conversation. As you build lists from these sources, consult your target ICP to separate the qualified from the unqualified.

People Who Visit Your Profile

People don't typically stumble onto your LinkedIn profile randomly. When someone views your LinkedIn profile, it is intentional because there is a level of interest. They are looking for something: There may be a trigger event that has opened a buying window, an incumbent vendor may have taken them for granted, or they might be in growth mode.

For this reason you should treat profile visits like an intent signal and immediately put these people on your prospecting list for follow-up.

For example, when Sarah noticed that a prospect named Michael had viewed her profile, she seized the opportunity to send Michael a message asking what had piqued his interest. Their conversation quickly turned into a discussion about Michael's marketing challenges, which ultimately led to a consulting opportunity.

To see the people who have visited your LinkedIn profile do the following:

1. Log into LinkedIn.
2. Click on your profile picture in the top-right corner.
3. Select "View Profile" from the drop-down.
4. Scroll down to the "Analytics" section on your profile.
5. Click on "Who viewed your profile" to see recent visitors.

You'll have a limited view of these people with the Free version of LinkedIn. For full capabilities you'll need to upgrade to a paid (Premium) account.

5

Job Transition Trigger Events

When a business leader transitions into a new role, they often feel compelled to prove themselves in the first 90–120 days. They'll move quickly to shake up the status quo, bring in fresh ideas, and implement new strategies—especially if they were brought in to fix problems. You'll want to capitalize on these buying windows.

This is also a prime opportunity to displace the incumbent vendor before they can reinforce their position. New leaders typically have no attachment to incumbent vendors or the old way of doing things.

They are looking for fresh ideas and better solutions, and they'll usually have the budget to make those changes. If you show up early with the right solution, you can position yourself as a trusted advisor and become part of their new strategy.

LinkedIn Free Version Notifications and Manual Job Change Search

You can keep up with job changes by tapping into LinkedIn's free notifications system and through manual job change searches. While the free version doesn't offer the same advanced tracking and filtering as Sales Navigator, it's still an effective way to stay informed when your connections make career changes.

How to Enable Job Change Notifications for Your Network

LinkedIn will automatically notify you when your first-degree connections update their job titles or move to a new company. To set up these alerts:

1. Go to the LinkedIn home page.
2. Click on the "Notifications" tab in the top menu.
3. Click "view settings" in the left column below your profile picture.
4. Click "Network catch-up updates."
5. Click "Job changes" and make sure that notifications are set to "on."

How to Manually Search for Job Changes

If you want to track job changes beyond your first-degree connections, you can use LinkedIn's free search filters:

1. Go to the LinkedIn search bar and enter the job title you're tracking (e.g., "VP of Sales").
2. Click "People" in the top menu to filter the results to individuals.
3. Click "All Filters" and scroll to the "Current Company" and "Past Company" sections.
4. Compare past and current employers to identify recent job moves.

Remember that a job change is a flashing neon sign that you need to move fast. If you wait until the leader is comfortable in their role, you'll be too late. This is exactly why you must track job change signals and take action *fast* with outbound outreach.

Job Change Alerts in Sales Navigator

LinkedIn Sales Navigator Job Alerts is a built-in feature that automatically notifies you when your saved leads and target accounts experience key job changes—eliminating the need for constant manual searches.

These alerts appear in your Sales Navigator home page feed, notifications tab, and email updates, allowing you to quickly identify when high-value stakeholders transition into new positions.

You can also use filters to search specifically for stakeholders who have changed jobs in the past 90 days, making it easier to build prospecting lists based on fresh opportunities.

How to Use the "Spotlight" Filter for Job Changes

1. In Sales Navigator, go to Lead Filters in Advanced Search.
2. Scroll down to the "Spotlights" section.
3. Select "Changed Jobs in the Past 90 Days" to filter for prospects who recently transitioned into a new role.

Save Leads and Get Automatic Job Change Alerts

1. When you save a lead in Sales Navigator, LinkedIn automatically tracks updates on their profile.
2. You'll receive real-time alerts when they switch companies, get promoted, or take on a new role.

3. This lets you strike early while they are still evaluating their new position.

In Account Search, you may also filter for companies that recently hired new VPs, CXOs, or directors and track companies showing buying intent through hiring trends, funding rounds, or leadership changes.

6

Leveraging LinkedIn Search for List Building

With a billion professionals on LinkedIn, finding the prospects that match your ICP can sometimes feel like looking for a needle in a haystack—but not if you know how to use LinkedIn's search capabilities.

Free Basic LinkedIn Search

The free LinkedIn search feature allows you to find people and companies that meet your ICP by applying different filters, including title, industry, company, company size, and job titles.

Accessing the Basic LinkedIn Search

The search is available in the search bar at the top of the LinkedIn page and on your first-degree connections page.

1. Click on the search bar at the top of LinkedIn.

2. Type a keyword, job title, or company name and hit enter.

3. Click on "People" to filter your search to individuals.

4. Click on "All Filters" to refine your search.

5. In the left-hand sidebar, you'll find multiple filtering options:

    a. **Connections:** Find first-, second-, or third-degree connections.

    b. **Current Companies:** Find people working at specific companies.

    c. **Location:** Target prospects in specific cities, states, or countries.

    d. **Industry:** Select industries that match your Ideal Customer Profile (ICP).

    e. **Past Companies:** See professionals who previously worked at key competitors.

EXERCISE 6.1 PRACTICE BASIC LINKEDIN SEARCHES

Stop now and practice the following LinkedIn searches. This will help you build targeted lists faster with less friction.

1. **Starting Line Search:**

    Start with a broad search of everyone on LinkedIn who meets your ICP criteria. Use LinkedIn's search filters to specify industry, location, company size, and other relevant attributes. This initial search will provide you with a comprehensive list of potential connections who fit your ICP.

(Continued)

(*Continued*)

2. **First-Degree Connection ICP Search:**

   Next, drill down on your list by focusing on your first-degree connections—those you are already connected to. These individuals are more likely to engage with you since there is an existing relationship.

3. **Second-Degree Connection ICP Search:**

   Search for second-degree connections, or individuals who are connected to your first-degree connections.

4. **Connections Search:**

   With this advanced search technique, you will explore the connections of a specific individual, such as a current customer or a trusted networking partner. By reviewing their connections, you can identify opportunities for warm introductions to decision-makers.

Sales Navigator Search Filters

LinkedIn Sales Navigator is a search game-changer. With its 20-plus advanced filters, job change alerts, and intent-based insights, it allows you to build lists that target not just the right people, but the right people at the right time.

With Sales Navigator you have access to precise targeting by deploying Boolean search strings. You may also save your searches and get alerts when new prospects match your criteria. This keeps your list fresh and relevant.

The platform provides robust filters to dial in on your ICP and target prospects precisely. Experiment with different combinations of filters, to refine your search approach based on what yields the best results.

Sales Navigator Lead Filters

Title: Filter by job title to identify prospective contacts with specific roles who are most relevant to your solution. For instance, seeking titles such as "VP of Sales" or "Director of Marketing" allows you to engage with those who can influence purchasing decisions.

Company: Use this filter to locate individuals based on their current or previous employers.

Company Headcount: This filter allows you to target organizations based on their sizes.

Company Type: Identify the type of organization—Public, Private, Nonprofit.

Geography: Narrow your search by specific locations, such as country, state, or city.

Industry: Selecting specific industries allows you to focus on the sectors most aligned with your target ICP.

Job Function: Filter by broader categories, like Sales, Marketing, or IT, to categorize roles without focusing solely on titles. This method enables you to identify a wider pool of relevant contacts.

Seniority Level: This filter is critical for pinpointing influential contacts and potential decision-makers within an organization.

Years in Current Position: Understanding how long individuals have held their current role can provide context for their organizational stability and authority.

Years at Current Company: This offers insights into loyalty and expertise, helping you gauge how well they know their organization and its challenges.

Years of Experience: Filter based on total career experience to identify contacts with significant industry knowledge.

Past Company: Use this filter to identify if stakeholders have worked for any of your current customers.

School: This filter can uncover shared educational backgrounds, providing an opportunity to create rapport based on shared experiences.

Profile Language: Target individuals based on their preferred language.

TeamLink Connections: This feature identifies individuals connected to your colleagues, which can facilitate introductions and strengthen your outreach strategy.

Connections: Determine connection levels (first-, second-, third-degree) to prioritize outreach based on the strength of existing relationships.

Posted on LinkedIn in the past 30 days: Focusing on active users opens the door to warming up cold calls through post engagement (likes, shares, and comments).

Shared Experiences: Identify prospects with common backgrounds or experiences, which can serve as a valuable conversation starter.

Groups: Filter by LinkedIn group memberships relevant to your industry, facilitating more targeted engagement with members.

Spotlights: Utilize this feature to identify individuals who recently changed jobs or have been in the news, highlighting timely engagement opportunities.

Personalized Alerts: Monitor leads who interact with your company for timely follow-ups or engagement based on their activity.

Buyer Intent: Identify leads demonstrating intent to purchase, allowing you to prioritize outreach to those most likely to convert.

Adjusting Your Search Settings

Once you've configured your filters, continuously refine them as you gather more data and insights. Start with a broad search and gradually narrow it down based on your prospecting outcomes.

- Use LinkedIn's "Save Searches" feature to track specific criteria. This enables you to revisit relevant leads and monitor any updates in their profiles.
- Keep an eye on LinkedIn's "Recommended Leads" feature, which uses your search parameters to suggest potential contacts. This feature can uncover leads you may not have previously considered.
- Regularly assess and reevaluate your identified leads to ensure they remain relevant as company structures and market dynamics change.

By strategically applying these filters and refining your approach, you can pinpoint targets and build robust prospecting lists setting the stage for successful engagement and conversion.

EXERCISE 6.2 PRACTICE A PEOPLE SEARCH IN SALES NAVIGATOR

Practice searching for key decision-makers and influencers in your target ICP prospects.

1. **Apply Job Title and Role Filters**
   a. Click on "Job Title" and enter relevant titles (e.g., "VP of Sales" OR "Chief Revenue Officer").
   b. Use Boolean search to expand results (e.g., "Sales Director" OR "Head of Revenue").

(Continued)

(*Continued*)

2. **Filter by Industry and Company Size**
   a. Click on "Industry" to select target industries (e.g., "Technology," "Financial Services").
   b. Use "Company Headcount" to refine company size (e.g., "51–200 employees" for mid-market).

3. **Target Decision-Makers by Seniority**
   a. Use the "Seniority Level" filter to target managers, directors, VPs, and C-level executives.
   b. Example: Targeting VPs and CXOs ensures you're reaching high-level decision-makers.

4. **Use Geographic Targeting**
   a. Click on "Geography" and filter by country, state, or city.
   b. Example: "United States" AND "New York City" for regional targeting.

5. **Use Spotlights for Engagement Signals**
   a. Enable "Changed Jobs in the Past 90 Days" to find new decision-makers.
   b. Select "Posted on LinkedIn in the Past 30 Days" to find active users.
   c. Choose "Following Your Company" to prioritize warm leads.

6. **Save and Track High-Value Leads**
   a. Click "Save Search" to monitor updates automatically.
   b. Save leads to lists for tracking job changes and engagement alerts.

Boolean Search

Boolean search is an advanced search technique that uses specific operators (AND, OR, NOT, quotes, parentheses, and wildcards) to refine and filter search results. It opens the door to more precise searches by combining or excluding keywords.

Mastering Boolean search strings in LinkedIn can help you get more precise search returns when the built in filters are not producing exactly what or who you are looking for. Whether you're targeting decision-makers, tracking buying intent, or filtering out unqualified leads, Boolean search gives you the control to create high-converting lists fast.

Boolean search works with both LinkedIn basic search and LinkedIn Sales Navigator.

- With basic search, Boolean strings are restricted to the search bar and cannot be applied to all filters at once.
- Boolean search is much more powerful in Sales Navigator because of the additional filtering options and intent data.

Essential Boolean Search Operators

Boolean basic search operators allow you to refine your search. Start by practicing the essential operators in search strings in Table 6.1.

When to Use Boolean Search on Sales Navigator

Boolean search in Sales Navigator is especially helpful for identifying specific prospects based on keywords or phrases that they use in their profile but that are not in their title. This is a highly

Table 6.1 Boolean Search Operators

Operator	Function	Example	Result
"Quotes"	Searches for an exact phrase.	"Chief Revenue Officer"	Finds profiles with Chief Revenue Officer exactly as written.
OR	Expands your search to include multiple terms.	"VP of Sales" OR "Head of Sales" OR "Sales Director"	Shows profiles with any of these titles.
AND	Narrows your search to include multiple conditions.	"Sales Enablement" AND "B2B SaaS"	Only shows profiles that contain both terms.
NOT	Excludes unwanted terms.	"VP of Sales" NOT "Marketing"	Finds VPs of Sales but excludes those in marketing.
(Parentheses)	Groups terms for complex searches.	("VP of Sales" OR "Sales Director") AND "Cybersecurity"	Searches for Sales leaders in cybersecurity.
Wildcard (*)	Searches for variations of a root word.	"market*"	Finds marketing, markets, marketer, etc.

effective strategy for identifying prospects that may not expressly fit the initial title-based criteria.

- Use a mix of job titles and industries, don't just rely one. Buyers in different industries and companies may have different titles for similar roles.
- Test different Boolean search combinations to refine your results.
- Save your searches and set alerts. Monitor new leads that fit your ICP automatically.
- Combine Boolean with Sales Navigator filters. Use headcount, geography, and job changes to improve targeting.

EXERCISE 6.3 PRACTICE ADVANCED BOOLEAN SEARCH STRINGS ON SALES NAVIGATOR

Stop now and practice the following 10 searches with your target ICP:

1. **Find decision-makers across multiple job titles and industries.** Instead of running separate searches for each job title, use OR to combine them.

    ("Chief Revenue Officer" OR "VP of Sales" OR "Head of Sales" OR "Sales Director") AND ("SaaS" OR "Technology" OR "Cybersecurity")

2. **Exclude irrelevant roles and industries.** Avoid wasting time on unqualified leads by using NOT to filter out roles and titles that don't meet your ICP.

    ("VP of Sales" OR "Sales Director") AND ("Software" OR "B2B SaaS") NOT ("HR" OR "Marketing" OR "Intern")

3. **Search for companies with high-growth signals.**

    ("VP of Sales" OR "Chief Revenue Officer") AND ("hiring" OR "expanding" OR "funding" OR "new office")

4. **Find prospects using a specific tech stack.** Target decision-makers who use your target technologies, increasing relevance.

    ("Sales Director" OR "Revenue Operations") AND ("Salesforce" OR "HubSpot" OR "CRM")

5. **Locate companies with recent funding or expansion.** Funding rounds often indicate new budgets and growth opportunities. This search prioritizes high-growth companies with fresh investment for your solution.

    ("CEO" OR "CFO") AND ("Series A" OR "Series B" OR "Venture Capital" OR "Funding")

(Continued)

(Continued)

6. **Target new executives within their first six months on the job.**

   ("Chief Revenue Officer" OR "VP of Sales") AND ("new role" OR "promoted" OR "recently joined")

7. **Find prospects based on LinkedIn engagement.** This helps you find active LinkedIn users who are already discussing your topic, making outreach easier.

   ("Sales Leader" OR "VP of Growth") AND ("posted about sales strategy" OR "commented on revenue growth")

8. **Find your competitor's customers and poach their leads.**

   ("Sales Director" OR "Revenue Leader") AND ("Salesforce" OR "HubSpot" OR "Outreach") NOT ("Works at Salesforce")

9. **Find prospects who recently spoke at events or conferences.** This helps you target industry influencers and decision-makers with high visibility.

   ("CEO" OR "VP of Strategy") AND ("keynote speaker" OR "panelist" OR "conference speaker")

10. **Find ICP prospects who are active in industry associations.** Members of industry groups are more engaged in their field and likely to be decision-makers.

    ("VP of Sales" OR "CRO") AND ("Member of AA-ISP" OR "SaaS Growth Association")

Saving Leads in Sales Navigator

LinkedIn Sales Navigator allows you to save your searches. This feature empowers you to manage and track potential decision-makers and influencers within your ICP accounts more efficiently because you don't need to recreate your search each time.

How to Save Leads in Sales Navigator

1. Go to the Sales Navigator home page.

2. Search for a company to view lead suggestions.

3. Under Recommended leads, click Save lead or Add to map.

4. On a lead's information card in Account Map, click Save.

How to View Saved Leads

1. Click Saved Searches in the top right of the home page.

2. A sidebar will open with all saved searches.

Running saved lead searches regularly helps you remain proactive, focus on new people, uncover opportunities, and keep your finger on the pulse of the prospects and accounts on your targeted list.

As company dynamics evolve, such as leadership changes, new projects, or shifts in focus, monitoring saved leads and accounts ensures that you capitalize on opportunities. This attentiveness also enables you to tailor your prospecting messages and approach based on the latest company insights, positioning you as a partner who understands their problems and challenges.

How to Add Contact Information to LinkedIn Lists

One major limitation when building lists on LinkedIn is that direct contact information is usually not readily available on your prospect's LinkedIn profile.

Highly effective fast prospecting activity relies on sequences of prospecting touches across layers of communication channels, including phone, email, in-person, LinkedIn DM and InMail, and even snail mail. But you'll need contact information to pull this off.

The problem is that manually chasing down contact information is massively time consuming and frustrating—time that you don't have when you need to move fast. The solution to this problem are sales data platforms.

Leverage Data Tools to Get Direct Contact Information

You amplify the power of LinkedIn's list-building capabilities when you pair it with a sales data tool that gives you instant access to contact information.

Most sales data tools have plug-ins to help you enhance your list-building efforts on LinkedIn. We're big fans of the ZoomInfo Chrome extension (Figure 6.1). It gives you contact information including phone, mobile phone, email, and physical address when you click on a person's LinkedIn profile.

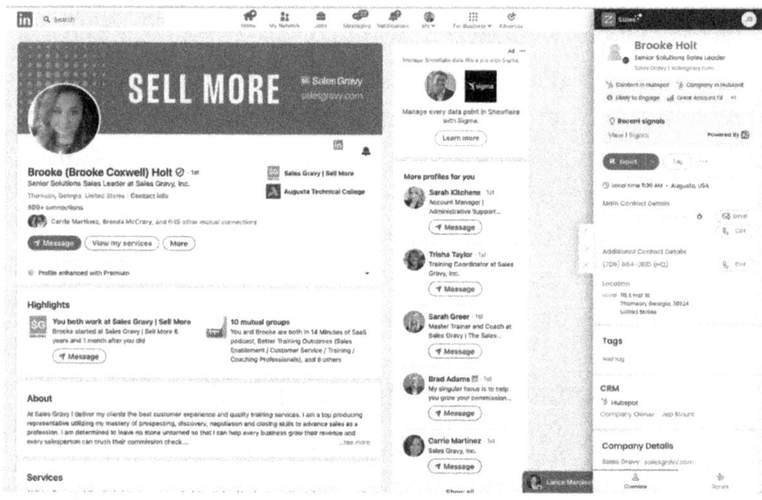

Figure 6.1   Sales data tools paired with LinkedIn's unmatched database transforms LinkedIn into the ultimate prospecting list builder.

With the extension you can:

- Export this information into a spreadsheet.
- Import the contact into your CRM and build a list there.
- Add them directly to a prospecting sequence in ZoomInfo.
- Identify other key influencers in the account.
- Get insight on signals to reference on prospecting touches.
- Call and email them directly from their profile on LinkedIn.

7

Prospecting Sequences

You've established your ICP. You've built targeted lists. Now it's time for the hard part. The moment of truth. You must connect with these prospects through outbound prospecting, engage them in conversations, and convert them into pipeline opportunities, fast.

The problem is that we live in a noisy world in which those same prospects are being inundated with prospecting messages from dozens of other salespeople who are also attempting to get their attention. So if you don't stand out, you lose.

But I doubt we're telling you anything that you don't already know. It's freaking hard to get attention, and it is not getting easier. There are days when it feels like you could be jumping up and down in front of your prospect in a pink bunny suit while throwing hundred dollar bills in the air and they'd still ignore you.

The Sledgehammer Approach Is Dead

One of the key reasons so many salespeople fail to break through is that their entire outreach cadence is pounding away at prospects through a single communication channel—typically a series of automated emails sent through a sales engagement platform like Outreach or SalesLoft.

Sadly, this sledgehammer approach just doesn't work anymore. Recent data reveals that salespeople are sending as much as eight times more emails today than they did five years ago and getting just a tenth of the results.

A big reason prospects are tuning out is that AI-powered sales automation tools have scaled email prospecting activity to an extraordinary level. In the past, crafting a single cold outreach email involved thinking and writing a message unique to each prospect. It was a slow process, which meant salespeople sent fewer but better prospecting emails that were at least tolerable for prospects.

Today, AI engines can create hundreds of cold email variations in minutes, embedding shallow personalization tokens to increase perceived relevance. However, as AI-generated prospecting emails flood inboxes, the very volume of outreach has eroded any impact from the improved efficiency.

Constant exposure to this irrelevant, repetitive outreach has left business executives exasperated. They are overwhelmed by the incessant barrage of messages and thus tune out, turn off, and ignore all prospecting messages—good or bad, human or AI-generated.

Break Through the Noise with Sequencing

The game has changed. To break through the noise and earn attention, you need to ditch the sledgehammer and pick up a multifunction Swiss Army knife. Multichannel prospecting sequences are that Swiss Army knife.

Sequences diversify your outbound strategies with a multi-channel, multitouch, interwoven-messaging strategy that helps you stand out and grab attention.

A multichannel sequence gives you the opportunity to meet prospects where they are and how they prefer to communicate. It also allows you to be creative with multiple iterations and formats of your message to home in on the one message that pulls your prospect in.

Key Elements of Effective Sequences

Effective prospecting sequences are a combination of targeting the right prospects, message relevance, and layering communication channels over multiple touches to build familiarity and systematize persistence.

Messaging

Message matters. It is the most important part of the equation. You need relevant messages that connect and compel your prospect to engage.

It is also the most challenging and time-consuming step. Poorly thought-out messaging or setting-it-and-forgetting-it with AI will get you ignored, deleted, and potentially blocked. This is especially true on LinkedIn where people are hyper-sensitive about spammy, irrelevant messages.

Therefore, it is crucial that you focus time and attention on developing relevant, authentic messages. (You'll learn messaging techniques and frameworks for crafting effective direct prospecting outreach messages on LinkedIn in later chapters.)

Effective prospecting sequences rely on a multichannel approach. These channels include:

- LinkedIn Direct Messaging and InMail (written, voice, video)
- LinkedIn Engagement
- LinkedIn Introductions
- Phone
- In-person (door swings, trade shows, networking events)
- Email
- Voice messaging
- Video messaging
- Text messaging
- Snail mail

If you are more comfortable with a particular channel—especially an asynchronous channel—shake yourself out of that comfort zone. The interwoven, cross-channel approach is crucial to bending statistical probability in your favor that prospects engage.

Cadence and Touches

The cadence is the order of your prospecting touches within the sequence, by channel.

Here are two examples:

- Phone > Voice Message > Email > LinkedIn > Video Message > Snail Mail > Direct Message (in that order)
- LinkedIn DM > Phone > Email > LinkedIn Video Message > Snail Mail > In-Person (in that order)

Once you've settled on the cadence in which the channels will be deployed, the next step is to choose how many prospecting touches you'll make per channel over the duration of your sequence.

Your touches should give you the highest probability of engaging prospects, while reducing the chance that you become irritating spam or harm your brand reputation.

Here are three examples:

- 5-4-3-2-1 = Phone 5×, LinkedIn 4×, Email 3×, In-Person 2×, Snail Mail 1×
- 4-3-2 = Phone 4×, LinkedIn 3×, Email 2×
- 3-3-3 = Phone 3×, Email 3×, LinkedIn 3×

The combination of cadences and touches are endless. There is no one-size-fits-all solution. Therefore, you'll need to keep testing until you find the right combination for your target ICP.

The real secret to developing hyper-effective sequences is testing, tracking, and measuring outcomes AND objectively—rather than emotionally—making adjustments to optimize your sequence strategy.

8

Integrating Soft LinkedIn Touches and Tags into Your Prospecting Sequence

LinkedIn is an invaluable communication channel in your prospecting sequence tool kit, but it requires a softer approach than other channels.

To put this in another perspective, if the phone and email are the boxing gloves of prospecting, LinkedIn is the velvet glove. It requires nuance, thoughtfulness, intention, and strategic thinking. With LinkedIn you are playing chess, not checkers.

There are three soft LinkedIn touches that you should integrate into your prospecting sequences:

1. Visiting your prospect's profile
2. Liking, commenting on, and sharing your prospect's posts
3. Tagging your prospect in posts

Warming Up the Cold Call

For many sales professionals, cold calling is the most challenging prospecting activity. If you are among these sales professionals, the thought of interrupting invisible strangers can strike fear in your heart.

However, using LinkedIn touches to build familiarity before your cold calls can boost your confidence, reduce rejection, and improve your outcomes.

Prospecting Lubrication

As the adage goes, "Attention is currency." When prospecting, capturing someone's attention is akin to striking gold. But when prospects don't know you, it's much harder to get their attention.

However, when people are familiar with you, it's like prospecting lubrication. It reduces objections and makes giving you time and attention feel less risky. Familiarity leads to liking. Liking leads to engagement.

The more a prospect hears and sees your name, your brand, and your message, the more familiar you become to them, and the more likely you are to grab their attention and compel them to engage.

Visiting Your Prospect's Profile

The easiest LinkedIn touch to add to your prospecting sequence is to simply visit your prospect's profile. If your prospect has LinkedIn notifications turned on, they may get a message that you visited their profile and they may be able to see that you visited. depending on their paid or free status on the platform.

We say "may" because there is no guarantee that they will get notified or be able to see that you visited. More and more, LinkedIn is reserving this feature for paid accounts. But it's still worth the effort because the time investment is literally just a few seconds and it's a super easy way to build familiarity.

As a bonus, if your prospect does see that you viewed their profile and subsequently visits yours, it may be a signal of interest to explore.

This is a good reason to ensure that you have your LinkedIn notifications turned on.

1. To manage notifications, click on "Notifications."
2. On the desktop version, click "Settings" under your profile picture in the left column.
3. On the mobile app version, click the gear symbol to the right of the search window at the top of the page.

To view people who have visited your LinkedIn profile on the desktop version:

1. Log into LinkedIn and go to your home page.
2. Click on your profile picture in the top-right corner.
3. Select "View Profile" from the drop-down.
4. Scroll down to the Analytics section.
5. Click "Profile Views" to see recent visitors.

To view people who have visited your LinkedIn profile on the mobile app:

1. Click the home symbol at the bottom of the page.

2. Click your profile picture in the top left corner of the page.

3. Click "Profile Viewers."

If you have a free LinkedIn account you'll see only a limited number of profile viewers (typically the five most recent visitors). You'll unlock the ability to see all of your profile viewers with Premium and Sales Navigator accounts.

Engaging with Your Prospect's Posts

One of the most effective ways to build familiarity with prospects who don't know you is engaging with their LinkedIn posts by liking, commenting, and sharing (LCS).

Let's be clear that this is not a one-and-done activity. You'll need to LCS their content multiple times over the course of your prospecting sequence in order to earn their attention and build familiarity.

It's also important to note that "liking" their content alone won't do the job. The motion is LIKE + COMMENT + SHARE. This is the combination that increases the probability that your prospect responds and engages during your prospecting sequence.

When you share (repost), choose the option "Repost with your thoughts," write a thoughtful introduction to the shared post for your audience, and tag your prospect.

Note that people can sense when you are just commenting to manipulate them and they know when you are being transactional. They can tell when you put no effort into your comment or copy/pasted it directly from AI. When prospects sense that you are manipulating them, they will not engage and they might even block you.

For best results, your comments and insights on reposts should be thoughtful, sincere, relevant, meaningful, and written by you. Avoid posts that are gratuitous and shallow. Avoid effortless AI-generated drivel.

When you demonstrate sincere interest in them and their content, you increase the probability that they will respond in kind and repay your interest with engagement.

Tagging Your Prospect in Posts

Tagging prospects in LinkedIn posts and comments can be an effective engagement and familiarity strategy. When you tag your prospect, if they have their notifications turned on, it is highly likely that they will see that they were mentioned and, out of curiosity, click to check it out.

If you choose to use this strategy in a fast prospecting sequence, you need to be very careful. Gratuitous tagging, just for the sake of getting attention, is considered poor behavior and can even get you flagged by LinkedIn for spamming.

Especially when you are tagging people with whom you do not have a prior relationship, you will want to be intentional, thoughtful, and limited. To avoid coming across as desperate and spammy, do not:

- Randomly tag prospects
- Tag prospects in posts that are blatant sales pitches or self-promotion
- Tag prospects in posts or comments that are not relevant to them
- Use tagging more than once in your sequence

Tagging works best if your prospect has previously engaged with one of your posts, you've had a prior conversation or relationship in the past (inactive customer or closed/lost deal), or if they have visited your profile. You'll get the best results with posts or shares about:

- Industry insights, research, or trends that directly impact your prospect's role or company
- A specific challenge that they have posted about or commented on publicly
- Something they've accomplished
- An article, video, or other media in which they were mentioned
- A subject that is relevant to their role and responsibilities

As a rule of thumb, if the content for which you are tagging them is relevant or truly benefits them, go for it. If there is any doubt about this or if it feels forced, do not tag them.

The tactic of tagging prospects is a much more powerful strategy with slow prospecting activity, but it can work with fast prospecting motions in a very narrow and limited strategic approach.

If you misuse tags, or overplay your hand, it can damage your credibility and push prospects away. So be careful.

9

Using InMail in Your Prospecting Sequence

InMail is LinkedIn's premium messaging feature that allows you to send messages to people outside your network (second- and third-degree connections), bypassing the need for a connection request acceptance first.

It is available through LinkedIn Premium and Sales Navigator subscriptions. Since you only get a limited number of InMail credits each month (one credit = one InMail), it pays to be judicious with how you use them and to whom you send them.

The Good

In effect, sending an InMail is much like sending a prospecting email, making it a valuable component of prospecting sequences, especially when you don't have a first-degree connection with your prospect.

The messages go to your prospect's inbox, and you can see when your message is read. This is a signal of potential engagement that can assist you with making tactical adjustments in your sequence.

The Bad

On the other hand, InMail has been overused for prospecting. It has lost a good bit of its impact value because receivers know that there is a high probability that most InMail will include a sales pitch rather than genuine communication.

This, along with inbox fatigue and an appalling number of generic, boring messages that lack relevance and personalization, has resulted in decreasing response rates as recipients approach it with skepticism.

Figures 9.1 and 9.2 are examples of bad InMail messages. As you read the first one, note that Jeb has been married for 31 years. It isn't a secret. He talks about his beautiful wife incessantly. A little research could have avoided this trainwreck of a message.

Do It Right or Don't Play

The first key to leveraging InMail effectively is getting real about its efficacy. It is not an easy button or a magic pill that will solve your prospecting problems.

If you are just going to send lazy, generic, spammy messages, save your time and go do something else. Make the intentional choice to either do it right or don't play.

The second key is using it for what it actually is: *a glorified prospecting email message*. It certainly has the potential to break through and compel engagement when it is used effectively. But that doesn't change the fact that it's just an email wearing fancier clothes.

Figure 9.1 A bad example of InMail. Jeb has been happily married for 31 years.

Let's begin with what *not* to do:

- Don't send salesy, hyped up, aggressive pitches, especially when they sound like your marketing brochures.
- Avoid generic messages that feel like a copy-and-paste job and lack real personalization, especially inane, AI-generated muck.

Figure 9.2 Another bad example of InMail. This message lacks clarity. Seriously, what is the point?

- Don't be vague about your intentions. If your prospect doesn't know what you want, why you want it, or what's in it for them, they are not going to respond.
- Avoid highfalutin (that's a "Jeb word") pitches using incomprehensible jargon—a word salad with no meaning.
- Don't waste your time with feature-focused product dumps. Your prospect doesn't care.
- Nor do they care about how great your company is or your list of clients.
- You are going to get deleted if you spell your prospect's name wrong. Seriously, you are on LinkedIn, so check it twice!
- Don't write long, multi-paragraph messages that cause eyes to glaze over.

As demonstrated by our previous examples, you don't have to look far to see that "compelling" is rare when it comes to prospecting InMails. The vast majority are awful.

It's baffling how often salespeople do zero research before firing off an InMail. Baffling because LinkedIn is a treasure trove of self-updating information about your prospects. Combine this with tools like ZoomInfo and AI and it's just malpractice to send an un-personalized, generic InMail.

Bad InMail destroys your brand equity, credibility, and image. It is stunning that so many companies allow their salespeople to disseminate this crap. Worse, the majority of sales organizations spend no time teaching their salespeople how to write effective prospecting messages.

How to Do It Right

Start with ensuring that your InMail is an integrated and planned part of your prospecting sequence. Your InMail message should be short, sweet, relevant, congruent, and interwoven into the other messages in your prospecting sequence.

And here's the good news. When your InMail message is good enough to get a response, LinkedIn will give you your credit back. That is a very nice reward for good behavior.

Though your ultimate goal is to book an appointment, sometimes it makes sense with your InMail to take a subtler approach focused on generating dialogue. Here are some examples that spark dialogue.

Provide Value

You can send prospects a relevant e-book or guide or links to articles, trends, industry insights, or posts along with your thoughts. Be sure that what you send is meaningful to them. This isn't about what you want them to know but what they want to consume.

Compliment Them

Likewise, you may consider sending a compliment, congratulations, or a note about a specific post they wrote, their company page posted, or something in which they were mentioned. You might also compliment them on a comment they posted or the courage to post it, if they took a controversial position.

Follow Up on Profile Views

If someone has viewed your profile, send a note acknowledging this: "I noticed you checked out my profile. I'm curious to know what sparked your interest." The objective is to create a casual segue into a deeper conversation.

Convert into an Appointment

When the objective of your InMail touch is to engage your prospect and set an appointment, then you will need a message that compels them to take action.

Before you write the first word of a prospecting InMail, consider your audience. Prospects are people, not robots. InMail should be authentic, personalized, and tailored to your prospect. Your prospect wants to know that you get them and their problems, so your message must be relevant to their situation.

The most effective way to tailor your message is to step into their shoes and ask some basic questions:

- What will get their attention?
- What are they worried about or focused on right now?
- What's important to them?
- What will cause them to engage or agree to a meeting?

The key here is taking time to do some basic research to get to know your prospect. Use that information as the foundation on which you construct your message.

The Four-Step InMail Prospecting Framework

The four-step InMail prospecting framework[1] is designed to give you the highest probability of grabbing attention, compelling a response (even if it is negative), and converting it into an appointment or a further conversation.

1. **Hook:** Get their attention with a compelling subject line and opening sentence.

2. **Relate:** Demonstrate that you get them and their problems with empathy and authenticity.

3. **Value-bridge:** Connect the dots between their problem and how you can help them. Explain WIIFM (What's In It For Me).

4. **Ask:** Be clear and straightforward with your appointment request/call to action.

Hook

You have less than three seconds to grab your prospect's attention. Your subject line must compel them to open your InMail. Once they open it, the first sentence must entice them to keep reading.

You've got to hook them. Kendra Lee, author of *The Sales Magnet*, calls this the "glimpse factor," that moment of truth in which your prospect either clicks to read or swipes up and moves on.

What's crucial to understand is that your prospect chooses to read your InMail for their own reasons, not yours. Therefore, your subject line and the opening sentence should be relevant to them.

---

[1] Jeb Blount, *Virtual Selling: A Quick-Start Guide to Leveraging Video, Technology, and Virtual Communication Channels to Engage Remote Buyers and Close Deals Fast*, Chapter 29 (Wiley, 2020).

A bad subject line makes your InMail feel like uninteresting spam. A well-crafted subject signals relevance and helps your message stand out in a sea of irrelevance. When your subject line aligns with your prospect's unique situation and interests, they are more likely to open your InMail.

Bad subject line: *IT Solutions*

Good subject line: *CTO—The Toughest Job in the C-Suite*

Your opening sentence should connect directly to and be congruent with your subject line—the two working together to compel your prospect to want to keep reading.

Effective opening sentences are focused on your prospect. Ineffective opening sentences are focused on you, your company, or your product, service, or software.

Bad opening sentence: *We are THE AI solutions provider.*

Good opening sentence: *Deloitte recently reported that the CTO has the toughest role in the C-suite because CEOs are pushing for faster efficiencies and savings from AI.*

Taking time to get the hook right will significantly increase engagement with your InMails.

Relate

Most companies and salespeople delude themselves into believing their product or service is so unique or different that it sells itself. If you are in this camp, it is time for a reality check: To your prospects, you and all your competitors look, sound, and act exactly the same.

Therefore, attempting to differentiate through a generic features dump makes you sound like everyone else and bores your prospect to tears. Here's an example:

Our world-class AI solutions keep you secure, up-to-date, and backed-up, whether it is desktop virtualization, cloud services, network security, or mobile device management.

What cannot be forgotten is that people make the decision to read your InMail and engage for their reasons, not your reasons. Their reasons are emotional. Your InMail will stand out from all of the other generic spam your prospect is receiving when you connect with them on an emotional level.

For example:

The CTOs I work with tell me that the increasing demands to integrate AI agents into legacy systems faster, while still keeping data secure has made their job harder and more stressful than ever.

Every human, at their core, wants to be understood. Thus, the easiest way to connect with your prospect emotionally is to demonstrate that you get them and their problems—that you can relate to their struggles and issues.

The key to relating to people is to step out of your product, software, or service and into their point of view. That's the beautiful thing about LinkedIn. Their point of view, frustrations, challenges, and experiences are on full display right in front of you. All you need to do is step back and do a little research before crafting your InMail.

Value-Bridge

Since prospects meet with you for their reasons, not yours, you must answer their most pressing question: "If I give you my time, what's in it for me?"

If you are unable to answer your prospect's WIIFM question with value that exceeds the cost of their time, your InMail will not convert.

An effective value-bridge connects the dots between your prospect's unique challenges, pain, and problems and how you can help them. Value-bridges differentiate you from your competitors *only* if they are relevant to your stakeholder. Otherwise it's just white noise, the same in a sea of sameness.

Bad value-bridge: *We're an award-winning, INC 5,000 fastest-growing company, and I know we can help you.*

As you craft value-bridges, step into your prospect's shoes and ask two crucial questions about your message:

- So what? (If it's not relevant to me, I don't care.)
- What's in it for me? (If it doesn't help me or solve my unique problem, I don't care.)

This is where your research pays off. When you know a specific issue that your prospect is facing in their business, you should bridge directly to that issue and how you might be able to solve it. If you are unsure of a specific issue, build a value-bridge to issues that are common to your prospect's role, situation, or industry.

For best results, align your value-bridge with your subject line, opening sentence, and relate statement.

Good value-bridge: *I work directly with CTOs in your situation, like your friend Dan McClane at GenTex, to quickly build a powerful security layer that gives you the peace of mind you need to deploy AI agents fast without putting your enterprise at risk for data breaches, hacks, and leaks.*

This is where logic intersects with emotion. When articulated effectively, in your prospect's language, your value-bridge will increase your InMail conversion rate.

Ask

To convert your InMail message into a meeting, you must ask for the appointment directly and confidently.

> **Bad ask:** *I'd love to learn more about you and any projects you're working on.*

In this example, the rep goes fishing. To your prospect this sounds like "I would love to hear the sound of my own voice as I pitch you on all of our wonderful features and tell you how great we are."

> **Good ask:** *While I don't know if we are a good fit for your organization, why don't we schedule a short call to help me learn more about your unique challenges with security and AI agent deployment? From there we can decide if it makes sense to set up a deeper conversation.*
>
> *How about next Thursday at 3:00 p.m.?*
>
> *If that's not convenient for you, I've included my calendar link below. Please pick a time that works best for your schedule.*

A few notes about this particular tactic. First, it disrupts expectations because you say that your solution might not be a good fit. That is exactly the opposite of what prospects would expect from a salesperson. Unlike pitching that pushes prospects away, indicating that you're not going to chase them pulls prospects toward you.

Next, you send a subtle but powerful message with the word "learn" (listen). This pulls your prospect in deeper because everyone wants to be heard. We love to tell our story to people who are willing to listen.

With the phrase "your unique challenges" you make our prospect feel important because everyone believes that their situation is unique. Finally, you take away the pressure by saying that if it doesn't make sense, we are not going to push things.

Then we ask assumptively ("How about") for a meeting and offer a day and time, which takes the burden off our prospect to make that decision. We also provide a calendar link so that our prospect has options.

EXERCISE 9.1 WRITE PROSPECTING INMAIL MESSAGES

Writing effective prospecting InMail messages is not easy. The most difficult step is training yourself to stop thinking about your product, service, or software and alternatively step into your prospect's shoes, relate to their situation, and learn to speak their language.

Develop the habit of researching prospects on LinkedIn before you write your message and becoming aware of what is important to and relevant to them. You will struggle at first. Everybody does.

The key is practicing until effective, authentic InMail messages roll off your fingertips. The more you practice, the faster and more proficient you will become at writing and leveraging AI to help you craft prospecting InMails that convert.

Start now by choosing three active prospects. Then craft an InMail prospecting message for each one:

Subject	First Sentence	Relate	Value-Bridge	Ask

10

Integrating LinkedIn Direct Messaging into Your Prospecting Sequence

LinkedIn Direct Messaging (LIDM) is an ever-evolving tool that gives you direct access to communicate with prospects through text, voice, video, images, and attachments.

The good news is that LIDM is free (for now). Unlike InMail, though, you may only send direct messages to your first-degree connections. (This is a big incentive to invest in building out your LinkedIn network, which we'll discuss in detail in upcoming chapters.)

Skip Past Gatekeepers

When you're moving fast, gatekeepers often get in your way. They block access to decision-makers and slow you down in your quest to set appointments and get information.

These days gatekeepers come in two flavors:

- Human gatekeepers that block phone and in-person access to decision-makers
- Technology and filters that decision-makers deploy in their email inbox to keep you out

This is another reason to love LinkedIn Direct Messaging. It allows you to skip past these gatekeepers and communicate directly with your prospect.

Fast Prospecting Use Cases

Like any communication channel, there are multiple layers of use cases. Over the course of this book, we'll introduce you to the various applications of LIDM. In this chapter our focus is on the fast prospecting use case.

For fast prospecting you'll leverage LIDM in two ways:

- **Indirect** prospecting touches that remind, educate, and build familiarity.
- **Direct** prospecting touches that interrupt, engage, and convert prospects into pipeline opportunities.

We'll show you how each of these tactics fits into your prospecting sequence and how to leverage them to get engagement. First, though, let's take a quick look at the LinkedIn Direct Messaging app.

Navigating the LinkedIn DM App

The first thing you need to know is that LIDM is always changing and evolving. LinkedIn loves to tinker with things. We are explaining the app as it is today, but it may have changed by the time you're reading this book.

LIDM is different on desktop and mobile. The mobile app offers more features and functionality than the desktop version.

Mobile Version

The mobile app includes features for easily taking pictures and recording voice or video messages directly into the app. You may also upload videos, images, and documents into your message and of course write a traditional text-based message that includes hyperlinks (Figure 10.1).

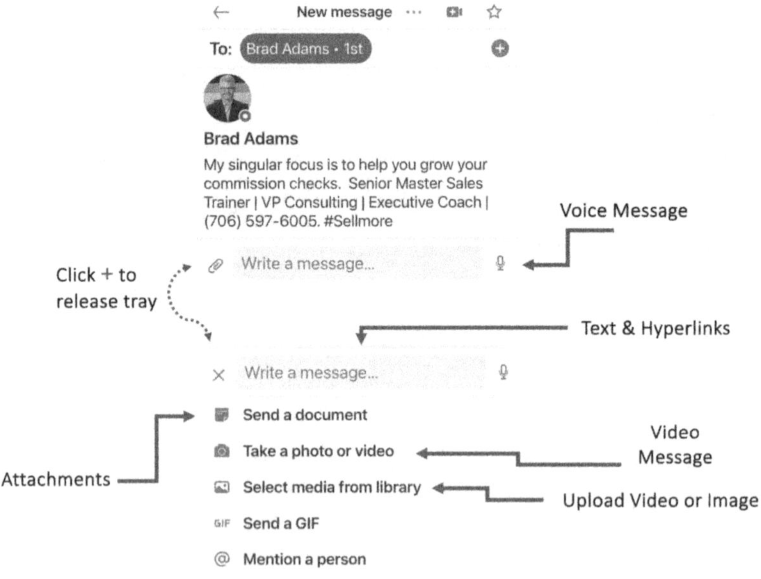

Figure 10.1 LinkedIn Direct Messaging mobile app.

Desktop Version

The desktop version, although not as feature rich, allows you to send traditional text-based messages that include hyperlinks and attach images, document attachments, and short videos that you upload (Figure 10.2).

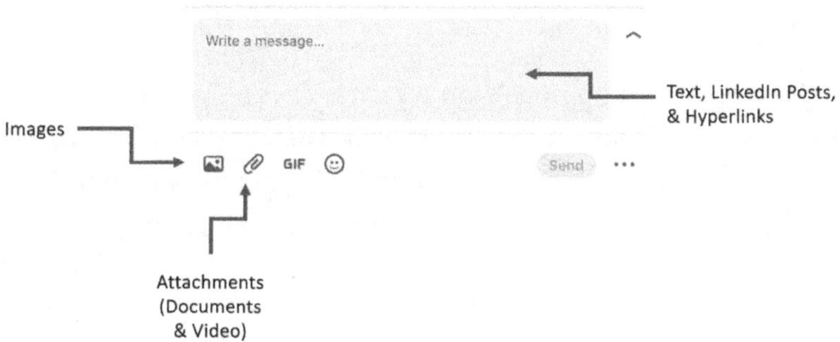

Figure 10.2   LinkedIn Direct Messaging desktop version.

A fun feature of LIDM is that both versions allow you to share LinkedIn posts—including videos—that will become fully visible and playable directly within the message.

Indirect Touches

LinkedIn Direct Messaging is a brilliant mechanism for integrating softer indirect touches within your prospecting sequences. These touches are focused on educating, reminding, and building familiarity.

Reminding

When you're running a prospecting sequence, it can be highly effective to send a message through one channel (for example, a voicemail) and then remind or alert your prospect that you sent the message via an alternate channel (for example, LIDM).

This doesn't need to be complicated. Your message can be as simple as this:

Brynne,

A quick note to let you know that I dropped something for you at the front desk of your office this afternoon. Enjoy!

Jeb

This *double-tap* approach ignites curiosity, compelling your prospect to seek out and read, watch, or listen to your previous message. A polite, professional reminder is nonintrusive, builds familiarity, and demonstrates that you care enough to follow up.

Educating

Leveraging some of the touches in your prospecting sequence for insight and education is a smart strategic move. When your prospects understand what you do, how you do it, and why it is relevant to them, they are more likely to engage.

This typically means sending your prospect a document, a video, or a link to resources including case studies, customer stories, white papers, studies, reports, micro-demos, presentations, articles, or podcasts. Brynne likes to share LinkedIn posts that support her case.

The challenge is that these days, people are very, very careful about clicking on links or opening documents from people they don't know. Most companies and email service providers, including Google and Apple, segregate these types of email messages into separate inboxes that your prospect may never see. Many emails with attachments and links are sent directly to spam.

This is where LIDM earns its paycheck:

- LIDM doesn't get caught up in spam filters or inbox segmentation.

- An attachment in an LIDM is considered more secure and trustworthy than one sent through regular email.
- Attached LinkedIn posts (perfect for videos) show up natively in the LIDM.

Because you're already a first-degree connection, if there's a question about whether what you're sending is legit, your prospect can easily jump over to your profile and check you out. If everything checks out, there's a good chance that they'll open your attachment or click your link.

Direct Touches

Direct LIDM touches are no different from any other fast prospecting touch. You are interrupting, engaging, and asking directly for an appointment.

Written Messages

Sending written messages is straightforward. The functionality is similar to InMail. For best results, your message structure should follow the same four-step InMail prospecting framework from Chapter 9.

1. **Hook:** Get their attention.
2. **Relate:** Demonstrate that you understand them and their problems.
3. **Value-bridge:** Connect the dots between their problem and how you can help them. Explain WIIFM (What's In It For Me).
4. **Ask:** Be clear and straightforward with your appointment request/call to action.

This framework works well with voice and video messages as well.

Voice Messages

The LIDM voice messaging function is an underutilized tool. Since very few people use it, it can help you stand out. When you send a voice message it grabs attention and breaks through the noise because it's novel.

People are naturally curious when they receive a voice message. Because human curiosity is a powerful force, they are more likely to listen than ignore it.

Unlike text, a voice message lets prospects hear your enthusiasm, sincerity, and confidence. An effective voice message is authentic and engaging. It feels like a conversation, which increases the probability of a positive response.

It's super easy to use—just push the microphone button on the mobile app and you're recording. The key is short and sweet: 30–45 seconds max. Make it personal and avoid rambling. Here's an example:

> **Hook:** *Hi Brynne. I loved your post yesterday on the power of social proximity on LinkedIn. It was super insightful. We even discussed it in our sales meeting this morning!*
>
> **Relate:** *It looks like you have a lot on your plate with running your company, delivering training, and traveling to client events. It feels like you're everywhere these days! It must be exhausting.*
>
> **Value-bridge:** *This is exactly why I'm reaching out to you. I specialize in providing fractional accounting services to growing training and consulting practices like Social Sales Link. We help you keep your financial house in order so that you can focus on the big picture.*
>
> **Ask:** *I have a short assessment to share with you that will give you visibility into any gaps that might be leaking profits. How about we get together this week and I can walk you through it?*

Video Messages

As a prospecting tool, video messaging is powerful and compelling, yet almost no one uses it. This is good news because when you use video, you rise above the noise and sameness and build familiarity. The more stakeholders see you, the more they like you.

Personalized prospecting videos make people feel important and show you care. You come across as a sincere, authentic human being rather than a faceless stranger. Stakeholders can see your body language, observe your facial expressions, hear your voice tone, and feel your empathy.

First and foremost, video messaging is about authenticity. Smile, have fun, and be yourself. Be human—no different than if you were sending a message to a friend.

The quest for "authenticity," however, does not mean that you can step over the line of professional communication. Recently a sales rep sent a video prospecting message that began with "Jeb, my brother." Total turnoff.

What's awesome is that the LIDM app allows you to shoot a LinkedIn native video and place it right into your message. You also have the option of shooting your video, editing on your phone, and uploading into the app.

Video messages should be personalized, relevant, and concise—30 to 60 seconds. Here is an example using the four-step framework:

> **Hook:** *Hi Julian (smile and wave hello). I hope you enjoyed the IFMA show. From your posts this week it looks like you had a great time!*
>
> **Relate:** *I can't even imagine how challenging it must be in your situation with so many maintenance projects on your plate. It's a lot to have going on all at the same time.*

> **Value-bridge:** *This is exactly why I made this video. I help multi-location property managers like you with a tool that virtually eliminates the need to waste time chasing down engineers and contractors for updates. My clients are getting 20–30% of their time back almost immediately.*
>
> **Ask:** *How about we get together on Thursday for a short call so I can learn a little more about your situation to see if this will be a fit? I have 2:00 open or you can click on my calendar link right below this video and pick a time that works better for you. Thank you for watching my video. Julian, I can't wait to meet you.*

LIDM Best Practices

Be judicious with LinkedIn Direct Messaging and follow these best practices:

- Don't overdo LIDM. Limit it to no more than two indirect touches and a single direct touch within any prospecting sequence.

- Spread out these touches and reserve your direct touch for the end of your sequence should other channels fail to convert into a meeting.

- Don't waste your prospect's time. Ensure that the information you are sending is relevant and high quality.

- Avoid using automated tools that blast your contacts with AI-generated drivel. This will get you blocked, removed as a connection, and reported.

Connection Request and LIDM Bad Behavior

When you're prospecting fast, having a challenge getting a prospect to engage through other channels, and you don't have a first-degree connection that opens the door to using LIDM, there will be a high temptation to send connection requests:

- As a direct prospecting message
- To get a connection request acceptance so that you can immediately slam your prospect with a LIDM prospecting pitch

Most people are smart enough to know that sending a "connection request sales pitch" is bad form. People who do this are either oozing with desperation, lacking social awareness, or just plain clueless.

To the recipient it sounds like this:

Hey there. I'm just going to come clean for transparency's sake. I don't really care about you. I just want you to buy my stuff. So here's the deal. Once you accept my connection request, I'm going to pitch you hard on how great I am, my company is, and product is. And then you'll never hear from me again. Are you in? Please reply now.

Do not do this! These tactics don't work and should be avoided. It's bad form, will hurt your personal and company brand reputations, and will get you blocked—closing the door on that connection permanently. LinkedIn connection requests should be used exclusively for slow prospecting activity (see Part 2).

11

Crafting Prospecting Messages That Break Through the Noise

*I*t is challenging to get attention when prospecting these days *because buyers are overwhelmed by the incessant barrage of similar-sounding AI-generated email messages filling their inbox.*

As a survival mechanism, buyers instinctively tune out and ignore salespeople. This presents a profound challenge: how to capture attention in a world that is learning to ignore you.

Persistence has always been a powerful ally to help top sales performers break through. But in this environment, persistence without differentiation just adds to the noise.

There are two primary prospecting message types that will help you differentiate and rise above the noise:

- Targeted
- Personalized

Targeted Messages

When you have a large prospect base combined with high activity expectations, taking time to research each prospect and craft a unique prospecting message before every prospecting touch makes no sense. It will completely bog you down.

To be efficient, you need prospecting messages that can be used for multiple prospects—one to many rather than one to one. The key is crafting messages that will resonate with most of the people and personas on your targeted ICP list.

Targeted messages work best with large groups of similar prospects, decision-maker roles, industry verticals, or product or service applications.[1] They are most appropriate when you have little information and the cost/benefit of doing reams of research isn't worth it.

Because this messaging is targeted to an ICP segment rather than to a single prospect, it will hit the mark with some prospects and miss with others. The key to success is crafting messages that have the high probability of connecting with the majority of the prospects you are targeting, causing them to feel that you wrote the message specifically for them.

Crafting Targeted Messages with LinkedIn

LinkedIn can help you craft highly relevant, targeted messaging—without the need for deep, time-consuming research on every individual prospect. When done right, you'll develop messaging that resonates with broad segments while still feeling individually relevant.

---

[1] You can learn more about crafting targeted messages in Jeb's book *Virtual Selling: A Quick-Start Guide to Leveraging Video, Technology, and Virtual Communication Channels to Engage Remote Buyers and Close Deals Fast* (Wiley, 2020).

Tap into Sales Navigator to create smart prospect segments based on shared characteristics.

- Start by analyzing industry and vertical trends to identify common challenges that professionals in your target market are discussing.
- Next, focus on decision-maker roles and functions, considering the specific pain points faced by your key ICP personas.
- Look for industry trends and hiring signals. These shifts often signal new business needs and open buying windows.
- Pay attention to geographical market trends, such as regulatory changes or regional economic shifts, that could impact their business priorities.

You can also gain insight into your ICP pain points from industry leaders and influencers in your space. Use LinkedIn's "Posts" search filter to see what professionals in your target segment are actively discussing.

Finally, join and scour industry groups for key signals. Pay close attention to the comments on popular posts. This is where people openly share frustrations, challenges, and opinions that reveal their most pressing business concerns.

Leveraging AI

AI can also do some of the heavy lifting for you with this research. Here's a simple prompt that works well:

What are some of the challenges that [ICP Persona] working in [ICP Company Firmographics] are facing in our current economic market?

The AI response is shown in Figure 11.1.

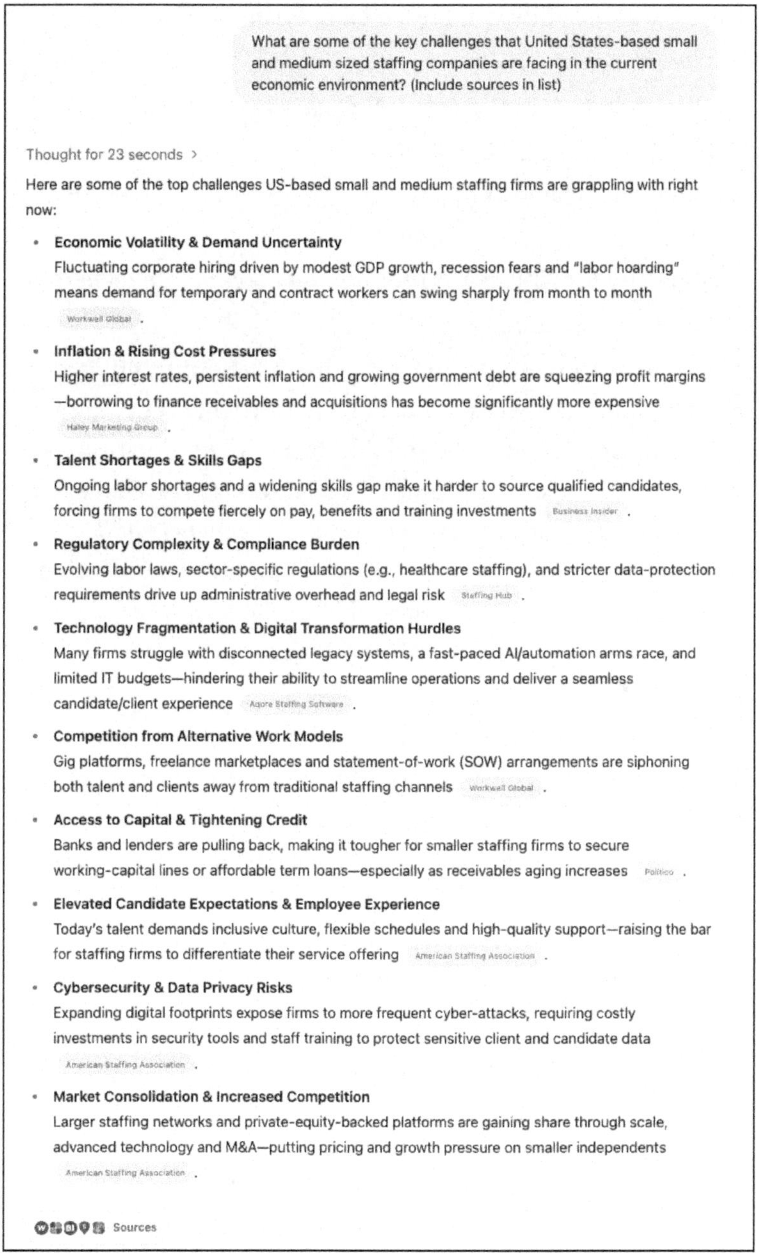

What are some of the key challenges that United States-based small and medium sized staffing companies are facing in the current economic environment? (Include sources in list)

Thought for 23 seconds >

Here are some of the top challenges US-based small and medium staffing firms are grappling with right now:

- **Economic Volatility & Demand Uncertainty**
  Fluctuating corporate hiring driven by modest GDP growth, recession fears and "labor hoarding" means demand for temporary and contract workers can swing sharply from month to month Workwell Global .
- **Inflation & Rising Cost Pressures**
  Higher interest rates, persistent inflation and growing government debt are squeezing profit margins —borrowing to finance receivables and acquisitions has become significantly more expensive Haley Marketing Group .
- **Talent Shortages & Skills Gaps**
  Ongoing labor shortages and a widening skills gap make it harder to source qualified candidates, forcing firms to compete fiercely on pay, benefits and training investments Business Insider .
- **Regulatory Complexity & Compliance Burden**
  Evolving labor laws, sector-specific regulations (e.g., healthcare staffing), and stricter data-protection requirements drive up administrative overhead and legal risk Staffing Hub .
- **Technology Fragmentation & Digital Transformation Hurdles**
  Many firms struggle with disconnected legacy systems, a fast-paced AI/automation arms race, and limited IT budgets—hindering their ability to streamline operations and deliver a seamless candidate/client experience Aqore Staffing Software .
- **Competition from Alternative Work Models**
  Gig platforms, freelance marketplaces and statement-of-work (SOW) arrangements are siphoning both talent and clients away from traditional staffing channels Workwell Global .
- **Access to Capital & Tightening Credit**
  Banks and lenders are pulling back, making it tougher for smaller staffing firms to secure working-capital lines or affordable term loans—especially as receivables aging increases Politico .
- **Elevated Candidate Expectations & Employee Experience**
  Today's talent demands inclusive culture, flexible schedules and high-quality support—raising the bar for staffing firms to differentiate their service offering American Staffing Association .
- **Cybersecurity & Data Privacy Risks**
  Expanding digital footprints expose firms to more frequent cyber-attacks, requiring costly investments in security tools and staff training to protect sensitive client and candidate data American Staffing Association .
- **Market Consolidation & Increased Competition**
  Larger staffing networks and private-equity-backed platforms are gaining share through scale, advanced technology and M&A—putting pricing and growth pressure on smaller independents American Staffing Association .

Sources

Figure 11.1 ICP trends.

Here are some additional targeted messaging AI prompt examples:

- *What are three major trends that are impacting businesses in the ________________ industry?*
- *What are executives in ________________ doing to cope with the ________________ trend?*
- *What are the five biggest problems on the minds of owners of ________________?*

Using the information you have gathered about trends impacting your prospect's industry, consider what they might be going through and how you might feel in their situation.

A simple follow-on AI prompt, like *"How do these challenges impact the emotional state or stress level of the owners and executives who operate these businesses?"* can give you emotional reference points for your message (Figure 11.2).

Find the Patterns

When you combine what you learn from LinkedIn with the information and insight from your AI prompts, you'll see common themes that appear repeatedly. Once you've identified these patterns, develop messaging that addresses the most common problems your target segments face.

For example, if multiple CFOs in a specific vertical are voicing concerns about forecasting inaccuracy, tailor your outreach to address that specific issue, rather than relying on a generic value proposition. This approach ensures your messaging is timely, relevant, and resonates more deeply with the prospects on your list.

A word of warning: Purely targeted messages, with no tailored personalization, are appropriate for high-velocity

How do these challenges impact the emotional state or stress level
of the owners & executives who operate these businesses?

Thought for 28 seconds ›

Owners and executives at small and medium–sized staffing firms often shoulder the weight of these volatile market dynamics alone. The result is a range of emotional and stress-related impacts:

- **Chronic Anxiety & Worry**
  Riding the ups and downs of demand, cash-flow fluctuations and economic uncertainty fuels persistent anxiety. In fact, 50.2% of entrepreneurs report anxiety as a top challenge, and 17% of small business owners say they consistently feel anxious or burned out founderreports.com   QuickBooks .

- **Burnout & Exhaustion**
  Everywhere "more with less" becomes the norm, leaders run on empty. Surveys show 34.4% of entrepreneurs report burnout, while 45.8% of small-business owners experience high stress founderreports.com   Truist Media .

- **Insomnia & Sleep Disturbances**
  Worrying about regulations, talent gaps and capital access often keeps executives up at night—30% of small business owners report trouble sleeping due to work stress Truist Media   QuickBooks .

- **Decision Fatigue & Overwhelm**
  Juggling compliance, technology upgrades and candidate shortages taxes mental bandwidth. Owners describe feeling overwhelmed by constant, high-stakes decisions—nearly half acknowledge stress is hurting their business performance Taylor & Francis Online   Forbes .

- **Imposter Syndrome & Self-Doubt**
  Rapid changes in technology and fierce competition can lead leaders to question their competence—31.7% of entrepreneurs report imposter-syndrome feelings, and about 84% of small business owners have felt like a fraud at some point founderreports.com   American Business Web .

- **Isolation & Loneliness**
  High responsibility and the stigma around admitting stress mean many executives feel they're "in it alone." Over a quarter report loneliness as a significant struggle founderreports.com .

- **Decreased Work–Life Balance**
  With 57% of small business owners describing a poor work–life balance, many find it impossible to "switch off," compounding stress and eroding personal relationships Truist Media   QuickBooks .

- **Fear of Regulatory & Legal Consequences**
  Navigating complex labor and data-privacy laws can provoke chronic worry—owners live with the fear that a compliance misstep could mean hefty fines or litigation Taylor & Francis Online   Forbes .

These emotional burdens can impair judgment, reduce resilience and, if unaddressed, lead to burnout or turnover at the top. Recognizing and proactively managing this stress with peer support, professional networks or executive coaching is critical to both the leaders' wellbeing and the firm's long-term success.

Sources

Figure 11.2   Emotions.

prospecting by phone, voicemail, and email. They are not appropriate to use with LinkedIn InMail or Direct Messaging.

Personalized Messages

When prospecting on LinkedIn, it is sales malpractice to use anything other than personalized messages. Why? Because your prospect's information, profile, and posts are right in front of you and being updated by . . . them.

When you send a generic or targeted message to your prospect, it's a massive turnoff. It demonstrates that you don't care and are lazy, and it makes your prospect feel unimportant. ("Seriously" they think, "you're on LinkedIn, and you couldn't even take a moment to look at my profile?")

Likewise, when the stakes are high and you need to grab the attention of a high-level decision-maker, a personalized message is the way to go on *all* channels.

In some cases, you may get only one shot to engage a C-level executive, so your message needs to be hyper-relevant. To break through, you must clearly demonstrate that you've done your homework and have taken the time to understand their unique situation.

Show Me You Know Me

Crafting personalized prospecting messages is time consuming. It requires research and a concerted effort to get the message right.

Still, everyone desires to be understood. Picture your prospect holding a sign that says, "Show me you know me." Before engaging or meeting with you, they need to sense a human connection and feel that you understand them, or are at least trying to.

Do the Research

Understanding your prospect requires research and effort. You need to put in the work to get to know what they are dealing with and how your product, service, or software can help them.

- Review their LinkedIn profile for what they are posting, liking, and sharing and leverage Sales Navigator to gain deeper insights.
- Analyze their LinkedIn Company Page.
- Listen to podcast interviews.
- Read news and PR posts about them.
- Read articles they have written.
- Watch videos they are in or have created.
- Research past activity with your company in your CRM.
- Set up Google alerts to have information about the company or individual sent directly to your inbox.
- Browse the company, division, and location through online searches, website, and press releases.
- Review their company website.
- Research trends in their industry.
- Research public information like 10-Ks and transcripts of shareholder calls. The best place to find company 10-Ks is the SECs Edgar app. (https://www.sec.gov/edgar/searchedgar/companysearch.html). For a shortcut you can Google "[Company Name] 10-K site:sec.gov." The best source for investor call transcripts is Seeking Alpha (https://seekingalpha.com/).
- Review investor relations communications. Just Google "[Company Name] Investor Relations."

- Make notes about jargon, core values, awards, trigger events, initiatives, changes, and problems that you can solve.

- If you share mutual connections, consider reaching out to those individuals to gain insights or even request an introduction.

AI PRO TIP

Deploying AI can drastically reduce the time and burden of doing this research and gathering the information. Google's Notebook LM (https://notebooklm.google.com/) is Jeb's go-to AI tool for analyzing the information you gather and making sense of it.

Using AI for Personalization

AI can speed up the process of research and gathering information when you are working on personalized messages. But be cautioned that AI does a poor job of crafting truly personalized messages.

- AI sometimes gets things wrong, leading to embarrassing, credibility-killing mistakes.

- Robot personalization, more often than not, is merely a shallow facade of personal facts scraped from the internet and social media platforms.

- AI personalization is often a combination of personal tidbits with gratuitous, sometimes cringeworthy, flattery, such as "I'm really impressed with what you are doing over at XYZ company." Executives easily see right through this and know that you didn't put in the work.

This is one place where you, the human, must put your empathy, intuition, and intellect into crafting the perfect message that relates to your prospect's unique situation, speaks their language, and shows them that you know them.

Stand in Their Shoes

Stand in your prospect's emotional shoes. Consider how you might feel in their situation:

- What causes you stress, worry, or anxiety?
- What frustrates you?
- How do you feel when you run out of time for important things?
- What do you fear?
- What makes you feel overwhelmed?
- How do you feel when you don't have enough resources to accomplish your goals? When does this happen?
- What might be stealing your time, money, or resources?

Use empathy to sense their emotions and acknowledge what they're going through in your message.

Speak Their Language

Language is powerful. Travel anywhere in the world and make an attempt to speak another culture's language and people will pull you in and embrace you—just for trying. You'll notice how little it takes. Even a few well-placed words can help you go from stranger to part of their in-group.

Language is the ultimate key to differentiation when prospecting. The human similarity bias causes us to believe that people who are like us are better and more trustworthy.

Speaking your stakeholder's language takes advantage of this. It makes your prospecting message sound familiar, safe, comfortable, and memorable. This gives you a distinct competitive edge in the war for differentiation. Your prospect's language includes:

- Company jargon
- Acronyms
- Industry terms
- Emotional hot buttons
- Pain and unique problems
- Opportunities and aspirations
- Values, family, school, and other areas of personal importance
- The way they express and communicate these things

LinkedIn is a window into what your prospect is thinking and feeling. You gain a glimpse into their pain, problems, values, ego, and aspirations. On LinkedIn, they teach their unique language.

Pay attention to how they describe themselves on their profile. Look for clues in their content and comments about their current objectives and pain points. This gives you insights into their priorities, values, and professional identity.

EXERCISE 11.1 CRAFT A PERSONALIZED MESSAGE

For this exercise, choose a high-value prospect that you want to get time with. Then using LinkedIn and AI, practice researching this person to find insights you might use to craft a personalized prospecting message. Your goal is to find five relevant pieces of information.

<table>
<tr><td colspan="2">Prospect Name:</td></tr>
<tr><td>1.</td><td></td></tr>
<tr><td>2.</td><td></td></tr>
<tr><td>3.</td><td></td></tr>
<tr><td>4.</td><td></td></tr>
<tr><td>5.</td><td></td></tr>
</table>

Next, craft a personalized message using the four-step messaging framework.

<table>
<tr><td>Prospect Name:</td></tr>
<tr><td>

Hook:

Relate:

Value-bridge:

Ask:

</td></tr>
</table>

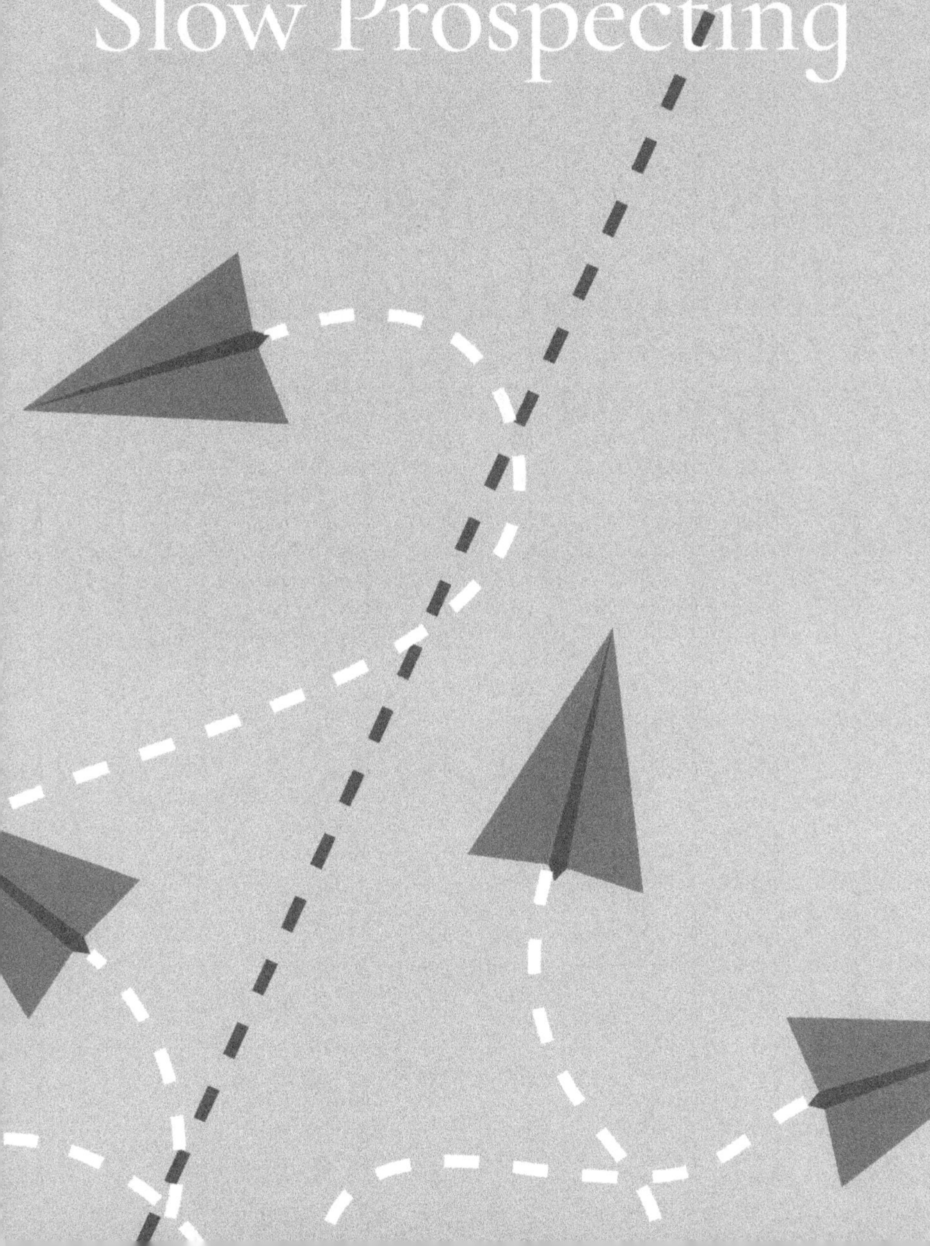

PART 2
Slow Prospecting

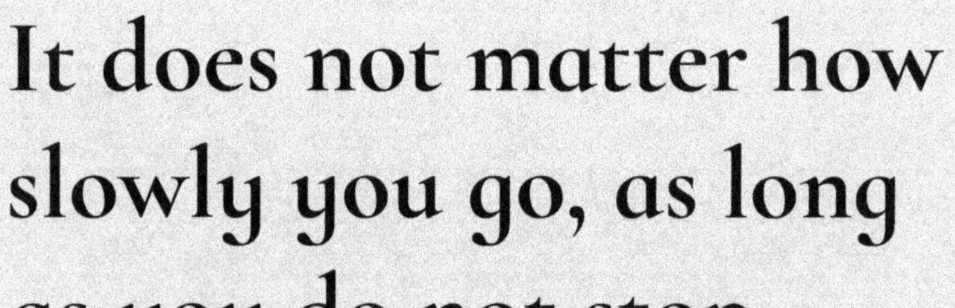

It does not matter how slowly you go, as long as you do not stop.

—Confucius

12

Familiarity

As Jeb wrapped up his final presentation, the decision-maker responded, "I love everything you showed me and feel confident that this is the solution we need to get our sales team back on track. Please send over the agreement." (Fist pump! There is nothing better than your prospect closing the sale for you.)

Then the decision-maker revealed, "What really blows my mind is how this whole thing came together. I've been following your content on LinkedIn for years. We've even interacted a few times. Then, when I was looking for help with my sales team, I sent your LinkedIn profile to my executive assistant to contact you, and here we are 10 days later doing business!"

Jeb's new six-figure consulting contract is a perfect example of the power of slow prospecting activity. His consistent activity on LinkedIn built familiarity and trust with his new client.

Then when the timing was right, and a buying window opened, his client did the work and contacted him. This made closing the sale much easier. In sales, it's as good as it gets!

The Familiarity Threshold

We've already used the word *familiarity* many times in this book. That's because it matters.

Familiarity reduces friction when prospecting. It attracts prospective customers to you. It makes it easier for people to trust you, which speeds up the sales cycle, reduces objections, and improves your win rate.

The primary objective of slow prospecting is crossing your prospect's familiarity threshold. This is the point at which a prospect recognizes your name, face, or brand well enough that engaging with you feels comfortable and normal.

It's the moment when you are no longer perceived as a stranger but as someone they know, recognize, and trust enough to engage with, seek out, and buy from.

Creating Fans Is a Slow Process

Think of your favorite actor—their face, voice, body language, and unique mannerisms. All these attributes are etched in your mind. You find yourself drawn to the movies and TV shows they star in, feeling a sense of comfort and anticipation each time, you see their name in the credits.

If you were to encounter them in public, recognition would be immediate. You'd feel starstruck, compelled to approach them and express your admiration or share how they've influenced your life. You'd want to ask for a selfie or an autograph.

But this emotional connection didn't form overnight. Your admiration for them developed gradually, shaped by repeated viewings of their performances. With each exposure, they became more familiar to you, elevating your appreciation until they crossed that all-important familiarity threshold. Only then did you place them on a pedestal and become a dedicated fan.

A True Competitive Edge

In sales, crossing your prospects' familiarity threshold gives you a true competitive edge because people tend to seek out and buy from people they know, like, and trust.

It's attracting, as opposed to chasing. It's the key to reducing your cold call burden and harsh prospecting objections.

Where there is familiarity, you'll find yourself engaging in far more meaningful conversations that lead to long-term business relationships. It gets you into opportunities sooner, before competitors even know what's happening, shortening the sales cycle so that you close faster.

A Soft Sequence

Slow prospecting is essentially a sequence of soft, low-risk interactions—without the sharpness of a direct pitch—that builds familiarity and trust with prospects, over time, through:

- Consistent, daily LinkedIn presence
- Thoughtful, personalized connection requests that do not contain a pitch
- Posting insightful, interesting, and engaging content
- Triggering their desire to reciprocate by liking, commenting on, and sharing their posts
- Following up in a thoughtful, natural, non-pushy way
- Helping, referring, sharing, and giving value without the expectation of anything in return
- Being associated with mutual connections, industry groups, thought leaders and discussions
- Investing in and building a strong personal brand

This is the foundation of slow prospecting—consistently adding value and increasing your presence so that when the buying windows open, you're already the obvious choice.

Just as you eagerly anticipate seeing your favorite actor in a new role, prospects will look forward to engaging with you when their needs align with your expertise, product, service, or software.

13

A Slow, Deliberate Prospecting Journey

LinkedIn has revolutionized the ability of B2B sales profession-als to connect and build familiarity. It is your most powerful partner for the patient, long-game approach of slow prospecting activities, including:

- **Connecting with prospects:** Turning prospects into first degree connections improves visibility and opens the LIDM communication channel.

- **Multi-threading and nurturing high-value targets:** Expanding relationships within targeted accounts and continuously engaging with valuable content and insights over time keeps your name top of mind when they are ready to make a decision.

- **Anticipating future buying windows:** Getting in front of identified buying windows by nurturing strong, genuine relationships and staying engaged with all key stakeholders prior to engaging them helps move the opportunity into your pipeline.

- **Developing a referral network:** Building a trusted group of professional connections opens the door to insight sharing, introductions, and referrals.

- **Personal branding:** Building a strong, credible personal brand establishes you as a professional who can be trusted to solve important problems.

- **Positioning yourself as an authority:** Regularly sharing insightful, valuable content shifts you from "salesperson" to a subject matter expert prospects turn to for guidance.

- **Creating buying windows:** Engaging in discussions and sharing content sparks curiosity, challenges status quo, and evokes awareness of problems, pain, and the need to change.

- **Educating and awareness:** Educating potential clients on the value of your company and solutions builds awareness through case studies, customer stories, studies, and data.

In a nutshell, slow prospecting is the process of weaving all of these activities together into a systematic and methodical process with the objective of increasing the probability that prospects engage and buy from you when buying windows open.

A Gradual Process

Consider the story of a young sales rep fresh out of college who connected with Brynne on LinkedIn. Over the course of several years, she followed Brynne's content and engaged with her posts. She attended Brynne's webinars, asked questions, and became a fan.

The rep did well in her first role and soon became a leader, earning a promotion that put her in position to influence buying decisions at her company. Brynne even congratulated her when the LinkedIn announcement of the promotion hit Brynne's feed.

One day, six months later, while in a leadership meeting, there was a heated discussion about how to get the sales team to use LinkedIn more effectively. That's when the young leader began advocating for Brynne.

She explained how she'd deployed Brynne's strategies as a sales rep and how it made her successful. Her influence on the group eventually led them to hire Brynne as their LinkedIn sales coach.

This story exemplifies the power of nurturing connections over time, and the reality that with slow prospecting activity there is rarely a straight line from connection to conversion.

Meaningful relationships take time to develop. It's a gradual process that requires patience. Slow prospecting puts you in position to win . . . once all the pieces come together.

Playing the Long Game

Slow prospecting is a fundamentally different approach than fast prospecting. It shifts the focus from interrupting and engaging to building relationships over time.

Rather than crashing in uninvited and interrupting prospects with a focus on generating immediate pipeline opportunities, slow prospecting is nuanced and strategic. It's about:

- Nurturing prospects and cultivating future opportunities
- Focusing on the journey, rather than the destination
- Playing the long game and setting the stage so that when prospects are ready to buy, they feel compelled to engage with you first
- Lowering resistance when you engage them through outbound prospecting

Systematic, methodical, and consistent slow prospecting activity is the gift that keeps on giving through inbound leads, referrals, and open doors to the hardest to reach prospects.

The Importance of Patience

With slow prospecting, patience and timing are critical. Being too quick to pitch can push people away. On the other hand, the failure to ask for a meeting when a buying window is open can mean missing out on opportunities.

Learning this balance is the most difficult part of the slow prospecting methodology. There is nuance here.

"Reading the room" requires both awareness and emotional intelligence—killer instinct combined with a soft touch. It's the discipline to pace yourself and deftly earn the right to initiate those discussions.

The key to gaining the awareness required to step into this nuance gap is detaching from the outcome. Detaching from immediate outcomes gives you the clarity to overcome emotional urgency and commit to a strategic, long-term approach.

In a way, it's slowing down in order to speed up. Slowing down to build trust, credibility, and relevance in order to speed up when buying windows open so that you lock out your competitors and close the deal faster.

A Dual Approach: Balancing Slow Prospecting with Fast Prospecting

It's a common belief among salespeople that slow prospecting is easier than fast prospecting because there is far less potential for rejection. This is why many salespeople abandon fast prospecting for slow prospecting—typically using the long-disproven "cold calling is dead" trope as their excuse.

Likewise, there are both salespeople and leaders who view slow prospecting activities as a complete waste of time because these activities rarely generate immediate results.

"I don't want my salespeople wasting time on LinkedIn" is a common refrain we hear from sales leaders. But this myopic mindset risks suboptimizing your go-to market strategy, and leaving money on the table in pursuit of only short-term wins.

We said this earlier but it must be repeated. The fast-versus-slow argument is a dead end. This is not a zero-sum game of one being better than the other. To be at the top of your game in modern sales, to sustain a robust pipeline, to sell more, requires that you become competent in the dual approach of combining fast and slow prospecting.

14

The Law of Cumulative Impact

Before we move forward, it's important that we have a frank conversation about the most essential aspect of slow prospecting: the discipline to invest time for LinkedIn activities every sales day.

The Law of Cumulative Impact is the principle that small, consistent actions compound over time to generate massive future impact. It is the incremental progress, persistence, and discipline of daily activity on LinkedIn that makes the magic happen.

For example, the LinkedIn algorithm (the hidden program that determines whether or not your posts get seen) rewards consistent daily activity. The more consistent you are, the higher the probability that your posts get moved to the top of feeds, earning you more eyeballs and attention.

Consistent, ongoing daily activity is even more important if you are just getting started with LinkedIn. In order to get real traction, you'll need to work relentlessly day in and day out for a year or more.

Randomness Is the Enemy of Effectiveness

Consistency is crucial. Interacting randomly and infrequently on LinkedIn is like tossing a small pebble into the ocean and expecting it to generate a wave.

However, you must be careful not to allow LinkedIn activity to take over your life because it can become all-consuming if you allow it to be. You'll need to pace yourself and balance LinkedIn work with the other impactful activities that drive immediate sales results.

Slow Prospecting on LinkedIn Is Hard Work

What cannot be discounted is that there is nothing easy about this. Slow prospecting is hard, grinding work.

- There isn't a clear feedback loop like with fast prospecting, where success or failure is transmitted almost instantly.
- You'll need to block dedicated time each day for LinkedIn activity and push through the desire to take a day off when you get tired of it.
- Slow prospecting is about faith that, by following the LinkedIn Edge playbook, you will get a return on your investment.

The grind of slow prospecting is real and can be exhausting. There are days when you'll be sick of it. This is why the majority of salespeople fail to get a high return from slow prospecting. They never stick with it long enough for the magic to happen. Success requires consistent, focused, and regimented discipline.

Time Blocking

Time blocking is a time management technique in which you segment your day into predefined blocks or chunks of time. Each block is dedicated to a specific task or focused activity.

Instead of working in a reactive mode, responding to whatever comes up, you're proactively setting aside focused time for priorities.

Your brain was not made to talk, walk, rub your belly, and chew gum at the same time. You simply cannot do multiple tasks all at one time and do them well. When you have too many things going on at once (especially complex tasks), your brain bogs down, and you slow down.

What your brain is exceptionally good at, though, is accomplishing a single task in short, high-intensity bursts. When you concentrate your focus on only one thing at a time, within a defined time block, you'll see a massive increase in your productivity.

LinkedIn and Slow Prospecting Time Investment

Limiting your time on LinkedIn to a defined time block forces you to be efficient and effective—getting as much done as possible, in the least amount of time, with the greatest possible long-term impact.

Without setting boundaries, it's easy to fall into the trap of scrolling endlessly, engaging sporadically, or wasting time on LinkedIn—spinning your wheels without any coherent strategy.

Short, daily time blocks (one hour per day is plenty for most salespeople) and the use of tools to automate certain activities are the keys to making the grind bearable. While an hour may not seem like much, the cumulative impact of daily engagement compounds over time, leading to a well-nurtured network, strong visibility with prospects, and more inbound leads.

Treat LinkedIn Like a Key Sales Activity, Not an Afterthought

LinkedIn slow prospecting must be scheduled with the same discipline as cold calls, follow-ups, and sales meetings. If you don't block time for it, it will either get ignored or become an unstructured, low-priority task that never delivers real value. Making it an essential activity in your prospecting routine ensures it happens consistently.

For best results, schedule a dedicated, nonnegotiable time block on your calendar for LinkedIn prospecting each day, whether it's 30 minutes in the morning and 30 minutes in the afternoon or a single focused hour.

Many people find that breaking LinkedIn time blocks into two or three shorter sessions per day—one in the morning and one or two later in the afternoon—helps them accomplish their goals while staying on track with crucial sales activities.

- **Morning (15–30 minutes):** Start by posting new content along with liking, sharing, and commenting on posts, sending connection requests, and responding to messages. This keeps your name fresh in your prospects' feeds early in the day. For example, Jeb schedules his morning LinkedIn work between 6:30 and 7:00 a.m. He uses this time primarily for posting, commenting, and sharing content.
- **Midday (15 minutes):** Focus on checking and responding to LIDMs and InMail. Respond to comments on your morning post.
- **Afternoon (30–60 minutes):** Send LIDM and InMail messages, connection requests, follow up with new connections, review profile views, monitor for trigger events and buying windows, check for prospect job changes, and engage targeted prospects.

During these blocks, set up a distraction-free zone to allow you to remain fully present. Turn off all notifications (including email and internal chat), close unrelated browser tabs, and set a timer to help you move on to the next activity when your time block ends.

Define Clear Objectives for Each Session

Go into each activity block with a specific agenda to maximize efficiency. Otherwise, LinkedIn can become a time drain with little real accomplishment. Each time block should have clear goals like these:

- Engaging with at least 10 target prospects' posts (liking, commenting, and adding value to their conversations)
- Sending three to five high-quality connection requests to ICP decision-makers and stakeholders
- Following up with all new connections from the previous day
- Posting one piece of high-value content to stay visible in your network
- Reviewing profile views and engaging with people who showed interest
- Following up with five people in your professional network

By structuring your time around specific, repeatable tasks, you will make steady progress, build and anchor relationships, and ensure that every moment invested in LinkedIn moves you closer to your objectives and a bigger pipeline.

For best results, batch similar activities together. Jumping between tasks is inefficient. This structured approach reduces friction and helps you get more done in less time.

Prioritize Engagement Over Passive Scrolling

Passive scrolling during the active sales day is a productivity killer. Every minute invested on LinkedIn during prime selling hours should be focused on high-impact activities. If you find yourself passively scrolling, reset and refocus on your defined tasks.

If you like to scroll to find relevant articles and keep your finger on the pulse of what's happening in your industry sector, do this at breakfast, lunch, in the evenings, and on the weekends.

Workflow Where It Makes Sense, but Keep It Personal

Some aspects of LinkedIn prospecting can be streamlined with workflow tools:

- If you have access to tools that allow you to schedule posts, it may make sense to use them for some of your content work.
- Use Sales Navigator CRM integrations to track LinkedIn interactions alongside email and phone outreach.
- Set up alerts for job changes, profile updates, and company news to identify warm outreach opportunities.
- Use Sales Navigator's Saved Searches and Lead Lists to stay organized and track engagement.
- Use AI where appropriate to help you with developing copy and ideas for posts and messaging.

15

Develop a Slow Prospecting Plan and Metrics

Slow prospecting on LinkedIn can yield impressive results if you have a solid plan. If not, you'll waste time on dark roads and dead ends. Therefore, before diving in, it's vital to establish a clear roadmap that works for YOU.

You have limited time and a quota to hit, which makes it crucial that you balance slow prospecting with high-priority sales activities that put immediate opportunities into your pipeline. With a good plan, however, slow prospecting on LinkedIn will become your force multiplier.

Set Clear Objectives and Activity Goals

Slow prospecting requires activity metrics no different than fast prospecting. You cannot manage what you fail to measure. These activities include:

- Establishing first-degree connections with stakeholders at prospective customers
- Building familiarity and relationships with stakeholders at prospective customers
- Identifying, anticipating, and cultivating buying windows
- Gathering qualifying information
- Generating inbound leads
- Opening and initiating sales conversations
- Building relationships with future prospects
- Building your personal brand and credibility
- Establishing thought leadership through content creation, curation, commenting, and sharing
- Expanding and nurturing your professional network
- Generating warm introductions and referrals

Begin with aligning slow prospecting and fast prospecting activities so that the strategies and tactics for achieving your number are all rowing in the same direction.

Next, define your slow prospecting goals as specifically as possible. Then create measurable steps to success and milestones that act as a compass to keep you on track.

Finally, break it all down into a structured daily plan that compounds your impact over time. Be realistic and honest about your capacity for slow prospecting activity. This will keep you from overcommitting yourself and then quitting when you become disappointed that you cannot keep pace.

Focus Your Plan on Targeted ICP Prospects

Your daily LinkedIn prospecting plan should be centered on a core list of target ICP stakeholders. These are the people you want to engage with systematically—building familiarity, nurturing relationships, and positioning yourself as a valuable resource:

1. Begin by mapping out your activity for the week.
2. Identify which prospects you'll focus on each day.
3. Plan connection requests and your approach.
4. Schedule time to engage with their content.
5. Follow up on previous interactions, and post insights that align with their interests.

The key to success is being intentional. Each of these activities should be preplanned, just as you would schedule outbound calls or meetings.

If you know which prospects are most active on LinkedIn, prioritize engaging with their content early in the week. If your goal is to grow your network, block time for sending connection requests and tracking responses. If you need to warm up existing connections, set reminders to comment on their posts before sending direct messages or calling.

Implement, Monitor, and Adapt

Once you put your plan into action, measure and monitor its effectiveness. Use LinkedIn analytics combined with CRM tracking to assess your progress. Focus on metrics you can control.

Prospecting metrics and goals can be broadly categorized into activities that you control and outcomes that result from those actions. While outcome goals are ultimately what you get paid for, they depend on the effective execution of controllable, measurable activities.

Process goals are the specific, tactical actions you take during each slow prospecting block. These actions might be measured by the number of new stakeholders identified, qualifying information collected, connection requests sent, LIDM or InMails sent, posts, likes, shares, comments, follow-ups, and other metrics.

When you develop your goals around the activities that you directly manage, you'll be more likely to stay on track and less likely to get discouraged by the things you cannot control.

Adapt your strategy based on feedback and results. Regularly updating your approach ensures it remains aligned with your objectives and keeps you in front of the right people so that when buying windows open, you are the obvious choice.

16

Managing Your LinkedIn Inbox

One of the downsides of LinkedIn for busy sales pros is that it adds another inbox to your day. Between email, CRM alerts, text messages, and internal chats, the idea of checking yet another messaging channel can feel like one more thing pulling you away from real sales work.

But since some of your biggest deals will start in your LinkedIn inbox, neglecting it is a big mistake. Managing your LinkedIn messages with intention ensures that you stay responsive to people and opportunities without letting it derail your day.

It's More Personal Than Email

Your LinkedIn inbox isn't like email—it's more personal, more direct, and often more valuable. It's where referrals land. It's where warm leads reach out. It's where prospects go when they've been lurking on your content and are finally ready to engage. And when that moment comes, they expect a response.

Time Blocking for Consistency

Just like email, your LinkedIn inbox can become a black hole if you let it. The key is setting boundaries and sticking to them. You don't need to be available all day, but you do need to check in consistently.

The best practice is to block a specific window once or twice a day, outside of prime selling hours, to check, triage, and respond to messages. For example, Jeb checks his inbox at lunch and again in the evening. That routine gives him two natural touchpoints without pulling him away from calls, meetings, or prospecting sprints.

Find what works for your schedule—then make it a habit. Consistency creates reliability. People begin to expect timely responses from you. And more importantly, you stay in control of your own workflow.

Prioritize for Speed

Not every message is urgent. Not every message deserves a response. Your job is to quickly assess which conversations move the needle, which require a touch, and which can be archived without guilt.

LinkedIn offers filtering options to help you sort and prioritize:

- **Direct connections:** Prioritize these first.
- **Premium members:** These messages often come from people willing to invest in outreach, making them worth reviewing.

- **InMails:** These can be spammy. Give them a quick scan, even if it's just to decline professionally.
- **Message requests:** This is where the junk tends to live, but every once in a while there's gold buried here—especially if someone's been following your content—so triage regularly.

Once inside your inbox, prioritize message responses into four categories:

- **Urgent:** Time-sensitive inbound opportunities or requests from prospects, customers, or referral partners
- **Important:** Relevant messages that move a relationship forward or deserve a thoughtful response
- **Nonurgent:** General networking notes, pitches, or cold intros you're not obligated to respond to right away
- **Immediate delete:** Pure junk and spam, no response warranted

You'll move faster and avoid missing opportunities when you triage and prioritize with purpose.

Move Faster with Message Templates

You want to avoid starting from scratch every time someone reaches out. That's inefficient. At the same time, you don't want to sound robotic or lazy. The good news is that speed doesn't have to come at the expense of personalization.

The solution is developing a small library of go-to messages for common scenarios. Start with these:

- Professional but warm thank-you for connection requests
- Brief, value-forward follow-up for new connections
- Polite, direct decline for unsolicited pitches or irrelevant outreach

- Template for sharing a calendar link without sounding impersonal
- Brief value response for someone engaging with your content

These templates give you a head start, but your job is to add context, reference something specific to personalize it, and keep it human. The goal is to sound like yourself—but in a faster way.

Keep your LinkedIn message templates, follow-up ideas, and CRM note shortcuts in one place that's easy to access. Use Google Docs, Magical, Notion, Evernote, or a CRM-integrated template field.

Integrating LinkedIn Messaging with Your CRM

One of the challenges of slow prospecting is keeping track of all the moving parts: messages, comments, connections and follow-ups. Without a system, things slip through the cracks. The good news is you probably already have that system— your CRM.

Most salespeople think of their CRM as a forecasting tool or a place to log deals. But when you're using LinkedIn as a prospecting channel, your CRM becomes a control center for tracking conversations, managing activity, and staying organized across accounts.

If you are fortunate enough to have a Sales Navigator Enterprise accounts, you can seamlessly sync key activities like InMail messages and connection requests directly into your integrated CRM, reducing manual data entry.

If you don't have a Sales Navigator account, you'll need a simple, low-friction way to log messages, engagement, and

conversations manually. Here are a few best practices to help
you do just this:

Use a Note Shortcut

When you have a meaningful LinkedIn conversation—someone
comments on your post, replies to a message, or mentions a
problem they're trying to solve—copy that into your CRM as a
quick note. Keep it simple. For example:

> *LinkedIn message 4/2: Katie from Redstone Services commented
> on scheduling headaches in the field. Replied with quick note
> and offered to share a short checklist. She responded positively—
> sent calendar link.*

This type of note gives you of note gives you context later. It
also gives your team visibility if you're working the
account together.

Drop Calendar Links into Your Messages

When a conversation moves toward a call, don't make it hard
to book. Use your standard scheduling link in the message.
It removes friction for your prospect, and it helps you track
meetings that come from LinkedIn activity.

Tag and Categorize LinkedIn Leads

Most CRMs allow you to assign lead sources or tags. Create one
for "LinkedIn" or "Social Touch." This gives you a way to filter
and report on how many deals or meetings originated from
LinkedIn conversations.

Set Follow-Up Tasks After Every Key Message, Engagement, or Intent Signal

Your CRM is brilliant at remembering important things, so you don't have to. If someone shows interest—even a small signal—set a task to follow up. Don't rely on memory or a list buried in your notebook. Drop a task in your CRM:

- *Follow up in three days if no reply*
- *Send article mentioned in message*
- *LCS their posts*
- *Reengage in a week if they view profile again*

If someone casually mentions a leadership change, a growth target, or a timing window, log it. These are the kinds of details that disappear fast if you don't capture them. You want to be the one who follows up when the timing is right.

Batch Update at the End of the Week

You don't have to log every little interaction the minute it happens. Instead, block 15–20 minutes on Friday afternoon to review your LinkedIn inbox, notes, and activity. Then update your CRM with anything important. If you've been consistent with social touches, you'll find a few worth tracking every week.

You don't need a perfect system. You just need one you'll stick with. Your CRM helps you stay organized and execute with discipline if you use it. Even better, when you feed it the right information, integrated AI will work with you to surface opportunities to engage prospects at the right time.

If you're serious about using LinkedIn to build your pipeline, then make sure what happens there also happens in your CRM. That's how you turn slow prospecting into a repeatable, trackable, productive part of your sales system and a reliable deal source.

17

The BTN Method

In James Clear's book Atomic Habits, *he talks about a strategy for making a habit stick: never miss two days in a row.*

In other words, if you mess up on Monday—if you skip your workout or drop the ball on your new daily LinkedIn habit—you give yourself permission to let it go. But get right back on track by Tuesday. You should never miss two days in a row and allow those mistakes to pile up and push you right back into the bad habit you are trying to change.

Clear's advice reminds us that we're all human. We're going to slip up. Life happens—kids get sick, you get sick, clients call with emergencies, your boss piles extra tasks on your desk, or your flight is delayed and you're stranded in an airport—sometimes you "just have to eat that piece of cake."

When this happens, give yourself a break. It's okay that you messed up once. Forgive yourself but just don't let it spiral downward by stringing together multiple days of misses together.

The BTN Methodology

But there is another strategy that works even better for staying on track with both fast and slow prospecting activities, makes it easier to bounce back, still allows for human fallibility, and over time yields far better results. If you want to build unstoppable prospecting habits and supercharge your performance and income, adopt the BTN method.

A few years back, Jeb was meeting a good friend for dinner. They hadn't seen each other in a couple of years. Chris was the CEO of a large company—constantly flying all over the world, dealing with high-level negotiations, board meetings, you name it.

We know from experience that this kind of schedule can wreak havoc on your diet, sleep, and exercise routine. But when Chris walked into the restaurant, Jeb was stunned. He looked incredible—like a completely different person.

Chris had lost weight and was in fantastic shape. As they sat down at the table, Jeb blurted out, "Wow, you look incredible. How on earth do you manage to find the time to exercise and take care of yourself like that with your insane schedule?"

The truth is that at the time, Jeb was really struggling with his own health. He'd been traveling without a break and gained far too much weight. He wasn't exercising, was eating poorly, and felt bad.

He was wrestling with all the typical excuses: busy travel itinerary, client dinners, lack of time in the mornings for a real workout, late nights in airports, book deadlines, and exhaustion.

Chris looked at Jeb, smiled, and said, "I use the BTN method."

Jeb instantly reached for his phone to Google "BTN" because he thought it was some new, miracle workout program.

Chris just started laughing. "You're not gonna find that on Google," he said. "BTN stands for better than nothing."

Why Doing "Just a Little Bit" Matters More Than You Think

Chris explained his philosophy: No matter where he is—no matter how jam-packed his day, no matter how exhausted he feels—he refuses to let a single day pass without doing some form of exercise, no matter how little.

On a good day, when he has time, he does an intense 45-minute workout. But if he doesn't have time, if he's been in back-to-back meetings from dawn to dusk, then he'll at least drop down on the floor in his hotel room and do five push-ups, or 20 jumping jacks, or a two-minute plank. Something. Anything. Just not nothing.

He explained that five push-ups is better than none and over time it all adds up. That's the BTN method—*Something is better than nothing.*

Getting Past the Mental Hurdles

One big reason most of us haven't adopted the BTN mindset is that it feels too small to matter. If you're used to a 60-minute workout, you might think, "Ten push-ups? That's useless. Might as well not do anything."

Likewise, if you only have time to jump on LinkedIn for five minutes because your day is so packed, you might feel that those five minutes aren't worth your time.

But the truth is that doing anything is infinitely better than doing nothing because of the cumulative impact of doing a little bit every day. For Chris, the months and years of never missing a day completely transformed his health.

Plus, BTN keeps you tethered to your routine, your discipline, your momentum, and your sense of identity as someone who always follows through and never misses a day.

Applying BTN to Prospecting

In his book *Fanatical Prospecting*, Jeb talks about how prospecting is one of those nonnegotiable activities you must do every single day to keep your pipeline full.

Yet, if we're honest, nobody really likes prospecting—fast or slow. It is hard, repetitive work. A grind. Exhausting.

We'll dream up any excuse to put it off: proposals that need writing, admin tasks, emails, that one big client who demands your attention 24/7, meetings, the boss, it's Wednesday, a full moon, or maybe just the allure of another cup of coffee in the break room.

Of course there are real, legitimate issues that impact how much time you have for prospecting and pipeline building during your sales day. You're busy. You have fires to put out. Big presentations. And a packed schedule of demos, discovery, and closing meetings. On those days when your schedule is that packed, it's not unusual to roll a zero and skip prospecting activities altogether.

But that's a big problem because those zeros add up to *zero*. Back to that brutal truth: The number one reason for failure in sales is an empty pipeline, and the number one reason why you have an empty pipeline is because you did zero prospecting.

The Law of Cumulative Impact

A zero day is a day when you do absolutely nothing toward your goal. In fitness, that means no movement, no push-ups, not even a single squat. In sales, it means ignoring prospecting entirely.

Zero days are the real enemy because zero days compound your inaction, leading to crash and burn failure.

By contrast, though, when you adopt a something-is-better-than-nothing mindset and commit to never rolling a zero, you'll accomplish more than you ever thought possible because you tap into the law of cumulative impact.

Even seemingly insignificant efforts—like making a few prospecting calls or LinkedIn touches—lead to major transformations in your pipeline, performance, income, health, and personal growth over time.

Something Is Better Than Nothing

Some days you'll knock out 20 meaningful LinkedIn activities. Other days you might only manage to make five. That's okay. Because five is better than zero.

By continuously stacking small wins, you harness the compounding effect and far exceed what can be achieved with occasional bursts of high effort followed by long stretches of inaction.

- Doing ten push-ups every single day for a year accumulates to over 3,500 push-ups. That's going to tone your upper body, build endurance, and keep your metabolism humming.

- Doing five cold calls a day is 25 calls a week, over 100 calls a month, and well above 1,000 calls a year. That's a massive chunk of pipeline-building activity from just five calls a day.

- Doing just three LinkedIn touches each day means that your targeted prospects see you almost 800 times over the course of a year. That's a lot of familiarity building.

Some days you'll hit all your notes. But for others, when you run out of time, you have to accept that doing something is a win because it's better than nothing. On those days you're aiming for progress, not perfection.

Adopt a No Zeroes Mindset

Start each day with the mindset that you are a person who never has a zero day of prospecting, no matter how swamped or frazzled you feel.

- Identify the simplest tasks you can do if you're pressed for time (like calling five leads, sending three LIDM follow-ups, or sharing a LinkedIn post).
- Fill the gaps in your day with activity. Always carry a prospecting list with you, so you're always prepared. Whenever you find yourself with a tiny window—maybe someone cancels a Zoom meeting or you have 20 minutes between appointments—use the gap for slow or fast prospecting activity. No chunk of time is too small.
- Celebrate small wins. It might feel silly to fist-bump yourself for just doing something, but that mental reinforcement works. You're rewarding yourself for no zeros.

And remember, this doesn't just apply to prospecting. Never let a day go by without some form of progress toward your sales goals. Five minutes, ten minutes, one micro-task—it's always better than nothing.

Greatness in sales comes from consistent daily effort. The pipeline is always flowing because you never stop feeding it. The "better than nothing" approach ensures you're always adding logs to the fire—maybe just a few some days, maybe a whole bundle on others—so you're never letting it burn out completely. Over time, that's how you create unstoppable momentum.

PART 3

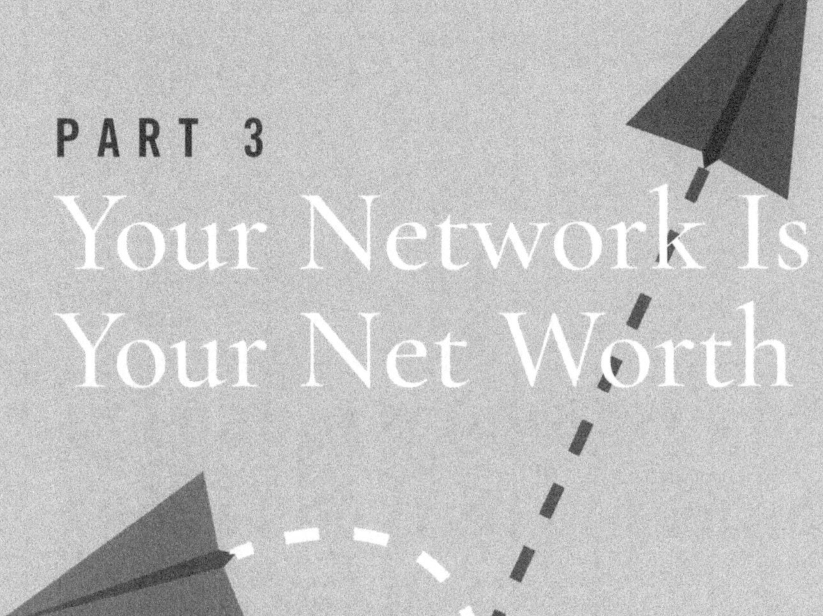

Your Network Is Your Net Worth

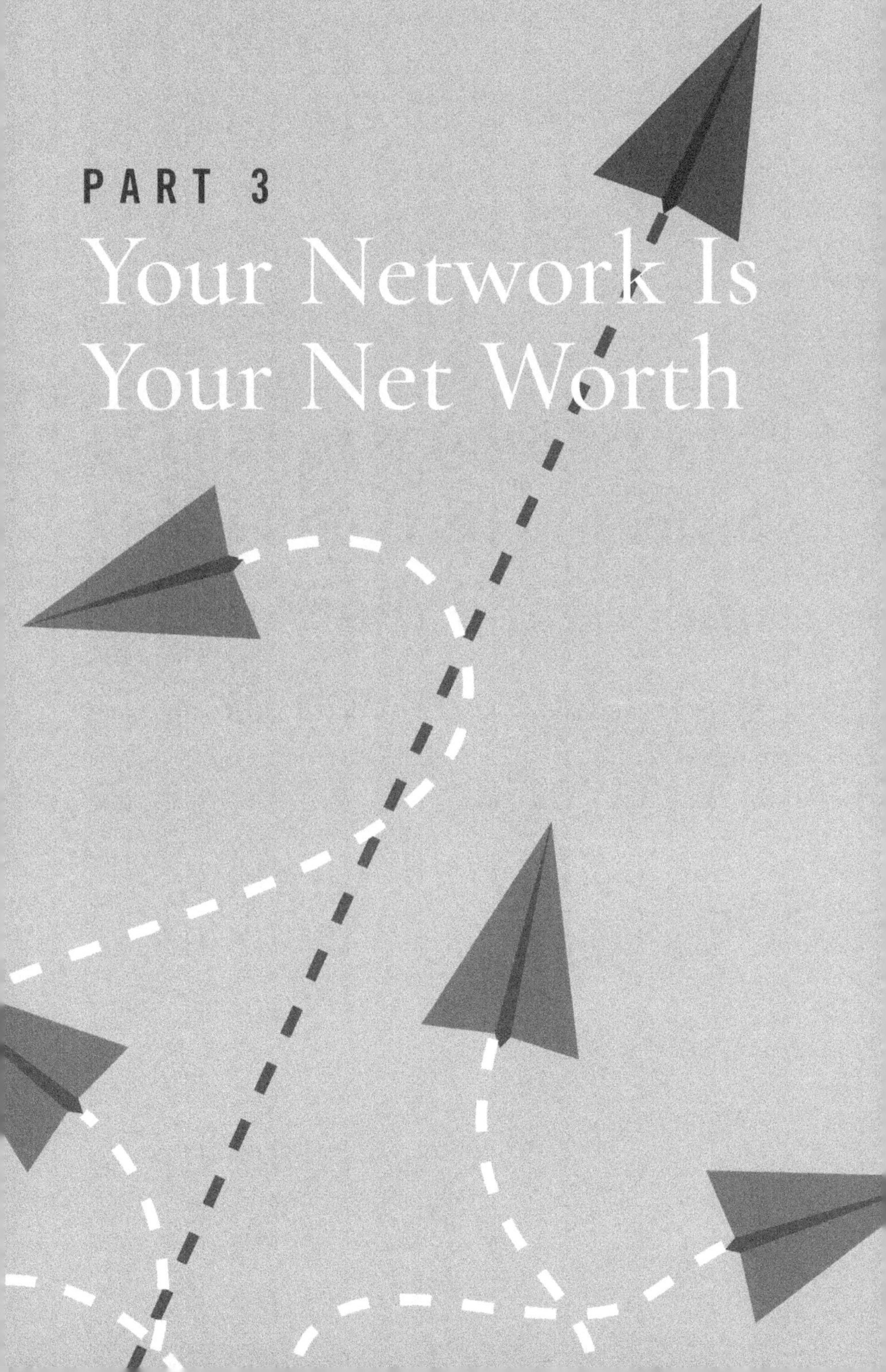

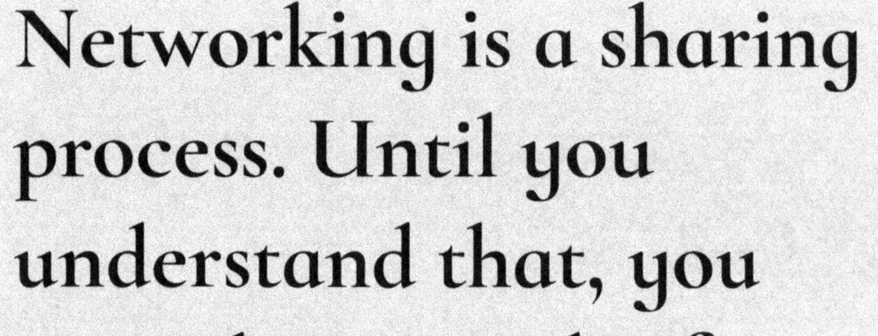

Networking is a sharing process. Until you understand that, you won't have much of a network.

—*Earl G. Graves, Sr.*

18

Your Network Edge

*L*ast year Ahmad, *an account executive who attended one of our LinkedIn Edge workshops, sent a connection request to Connor, the director of facilities services at a large logistics company that was on his targeted list.*

There was no immediate opportunity. No pitch. Just a well-written connection request, which Connor accepted.

Ahmad followed up by monitoring Connor's posts, liking and commenting when appropriate. On one occasion, Ahmad sent Connor a LinkedIn Direct Message (LIDM) with a link to an article on how AI was being integrated into facility management services. Connor thanked him but there was no further discussion.

Meanwhile, Ahmad was actively posting and sharing regular content on his own feed. Much of it focused on leveraging technology and AI to reduce costs by making large facilities and warehouses more energy efficient.

Six months later, out of nowhere, Connor sent Ahmad an LIDM asking for a meeting. His company had just been acquired by a private equity company. He was getting pressure to reduce costs fast and wanted to learn more about Ahmad's technology.

- Because Connor was a first-degree connection, every time he opened LinkedIn, Ahmad's name and posts kept showing up in his feed. And when a trigger event opened up a buying window, Connor was able to connect with Ahmad easily through LIDM.

- Connor initiated the conversation with Ahmad because he was familiar and had built credibility. Ahmad closed the deal in less than 30 days. Because his solution was so successful for Connor, Ahmad now works with three other companies in the private equity group's portfolio.

The Heart of It All

There's little doubt that you've heard this old saying: *Your network is your net worth.* Is it overused? Maybe. But that doesn't make it any less true.

In sales, your network determines your reach, your influence, and ultimately your sales results. In today's world, that starts with adopting a winning LinkedIn networking strategy.

Ahmad's story illustrates why systematically building your LinkedIn network is at the heart of a successful slow prospecting strategy. A well-built LinkedIn network works quietly in the background until the time is right. Then it's game on.

Let's begin our discussion by exploring the three types of connectors and network builders on the LinkedIn platform.

LION (LinkedIn Open Networker)

LIONs accept connection requests from everyone and anyone, usually prioritizing quantity over quality. LIONs tend to have thousands of connections, but they don't really know anyone in their network because it is a thousand miles wide and only an inch deep.

Purist

The purist connects only with people they know personally. They have an extreme focus on quality over quantity. Their network makeup is the opposite of the LION—an inch wide and a thousand miles deep.

Strategic Networker

Strategic networkers build and optimize their network to align with their overarching sales and business objectives. They connect strategically with prospects, centers of influence, key thought leaders, and professionals who can make connections and provide referrals. Their network is a well-designed balance of depth and width.

Be a Strategic and Targeted Networker

Strategic networking makes the most sense in sales because it helps you squeeze the most value from your network by building mutually beneficial connections. The more targeted and intentional your network, the easier it becomes to get referrals, open doors, close deals, and help people.

LinkedIn gives you access to decision-makers, influencers, connectors, referrers, and peers—but only if you've built the right network in the first place. When your connections reflect the market you serve, and when the people in your network are the same people who buy, refer, or influence deals, everything gets easier:

- Your content lands with the right audience.
- Your profile attracts the right attention.
- Your messages spark the right responses.

- Conversations aren't forced and contrived.
- LIDM becomes a powerful communication tool for doing business.

The truth is that the more targeted your network, the more sales you'll make. That's why investing time, attention, and effort into building your LinkedIn network is like putting money in the bank.

Network Levers

There are two crucial levers you must pull to build a powerful, productive, and profitable LinkedIn network and conduct effective slow prospecting.

Prospects

First, you must connect strategically with prospects that match your Ideal Customer Profile (ICP), ensuring that your network is filled with the decision-makers, influencers, and key stakeholders who drive buying decisions.

It's about multi-threading your way through an organization, establishing relationships at different levels to create influence, shorten sales cycles, and reduce deal risk.

Professionals

Second, you need to build a network of professional allies—people who can refer business to you and to whom you can refer business in return. It's about methodically engineering social proximity—viewing your LinkedIn professional network as a series of connections that lead to your target.

With this mindset, you are building a network that includes industry peers, consultants, vendors, and trusted advisors who share common client bases and can open doors you wouldn't be able to reach on your own.

Top sales professionals connect, contribute, and facilitate value exchanges with their professional network that create more opportunities for everyone.

Your Network Is a Sales Safety Net

Building your network is a slow, deliberate process. You may not see the payoff immediately. But over time, your network compounds in value. The relationships grow. Your influence expands. The leads and referrals show up. And when you really need it—when the pipeline is thin or a deal falls through—your network becomes the safety net that catches you.

19

The Seven People You Need in Your Network

A strong LinkedIn network is not built by chance. It is engineered with intent. It's not about accumulating thousands of shallow connections, it's about targeting strategic relationships that align with your sales objectives and goals.

There are seven types of people who you need in your network:

1. Decision-makers and influencers from targeted ICP companies
2. Key contacts from existing accounts
3. Key contacts within your channel partners and distributors
4. Key vendors and suppliers

5. Referral partners and connectors

6. Thought leaders, industry experts, and influencers

7. Peers and colleagues inside your company or organization

Decision-Makers and Key Influencers in Your ICP

Your highest-priority connections should be the key decision-makers and influencers within your list of targeted ICP prospects. This is your multi-thread—the people who have the influence to shape buying decisions, the insider information to coach and introduce you to other stakeholders, the budget to buy, or the authority to say yes.

When these people are part of your LinkedIn network, it reduces prospecting friction and provides invaluable sales intelligence that helps you:

- Gain real-time insight into their challenges, priorities, and mindset.

- Know when a prospect is struggling with a problem you can solve.

- See buying signals before they become obvious.

- Notice when key decision-makers and influencers change jobs, take on new initiatives, or shift strategies—giving you the inside track on new opportunities before your competitors are even aware.

Existing Customers

Maintaining a network of key people within your existing customer base is a key to driving account expansion, getting renewals, and deepening customer relationships to improve retention.

Customer connections give you ongoing visibility into internal changes, new initiatives, and shifts in priorities that could open the door for upsell and cross-sell opportunities.

They also serve as social proof. When potential buyers see that you're already connected to companies like theirs—or to individuals they respect in their industry—it validates your expertise and creates an immediate sense of trust. Prospects feel more comfortable engaging with someone who's already doing business with people in their world.

But it's not enough to just connect with one or two champions inside an account and call it a day. If you're only connected to one person in an account, and that person leaves, your influence leaves with them. Adding to your connections increases your stickiness, reduces risk, and protects your position when key stakeholders move on.

Engage, celebrate their wins, stay visible, and invest in the relationship. Your existing customers are often your best source of introductions to other divisions, subsidiaries, or even peer companies in their network. But you won't get those referrals if you're not staying top of mind.

Your customer contacts are also your best advocates. Happy customers are willing to vouch for you, introduce you to their peers, and provide testimonials that carry weight with future buyers. When managed correctly, these connections don't just help you protect and grow existing accounts—they turn your customers into a competitive advantage.

Channel Partners and Distributors

If you sell through channel partners, distributors, or resellers, building and maintaining strong connections with these stakeholders is nonnegotiable. Your channel partners are an extension of your sales team—representing your brand, driving revenue, and influencing how your product is perceived in the market. The stronger your relationships with these partners, the more effectively they'll advocate for you.

When your partners trust you, they're more likely to bring you into high-stakes opportunities, advocate for your solution over competing options, and share warm introductions that open doors with key accounts.

When adding channel partners and distributors to your network, focus on:

- Account managers, sales leaders, and customer success teams.
- Executives who influence channel strategy and resource allocation.
- Field reps who engage directly with your target customers.

The stronger your relationships with these partners, the more influence you'll have—and the more deals you'll close.

Vendors and Suppliers

Vendors and suppliers play a critical role in the success of your business, but they're often overlooked when it comes to LinkedIn networking. These are the people who support your customers, enhance your product or service offering, or provide essential components that make your solution stronger.

These connections keep you plugged into industry trends, market shifts, and emerging technologies that can give you an edge in conversations with prospects. When you're aware of innovations or changes in your supply chain or partner ecosystem, you can proactively share insights with customers, reinforcing your position as a trusted advisor.

Vendors and suppliers are often connected to the same decision-makers and influencers you're targeting. They have relationships you can leverage, and in many cases, they're in a position to refer or introduce you to high-value prospects. These warm introductions create familiarity and credibility that shortens sales cycles and accelerates pipeline velocity.

Referral Partners and Connectors

Among the most profitable relationships in your network are the connectors who can bridge the familiarity gap with warm introductions and referrals that get you into the door faster and with more credibility than cold outreach.

When adding connectors to your network, focus on:

- Consultants and training service providers in your industry
- Business coaches, advisors, professional service providers or investors who work with your target audience
- Sales reps from complementary industries who target the same buyers
- Friends and connections from your time at college or university

Industry Thought Leaders and Experts

Expanding your network with industry experts and influencers gives you access to market insights, best practices, and potential collaborations. These relationships help you stay ahead of industry trends, sharpen your sales skills, burnish your personal brand and visibility, help you with important insights, and new sales strategies. These connections may include:

- Trade association leaders
- Industry training specialists
- Consultants
- Experts, thought leaders, and influencers

Colleagues and Internal Team Members

Your LinkedIn network should also include the people you work with—both inside and outside your direct sales team. A strong internal network helps you stay informed on company updates, share key content, and leverage mutual connections.

Down the road, these connections may help you with leads, referrals, introduction, references, and career opportunities, so staying in touch matters.

Align Your Network to Your Sales Objectives

When you ensure that every new connection that you initiate or allow in is a member of one of these seven groups, you will build a network that is aligned with your core sales objectives.

20

Optimizing and Refining Your Existing LinkedIn Network

When it comes to building a winning LinkedIn network, most people aren't starting from scratch. You've already built a network of connections. The question is, are you getting the maximum return on your existing network?

Over time, our LinkedIn networks tend to drift away from the center of our target. We end up connected to people who no longer align with our sales objectives. When this happens, your network becomes more noise than value.

To fix this problem, you'll need to take a step back to analyze your connections to ensure your network is optimized for where you're going—not where you've been. You'll do this by systematically removing unnecessary and low-value connections while closing the gaps in your network with new connections that are better aligned with your sales and account expansion objectives.

Get a List of Your Current Connections

The first step is to analyze who is already in your network. Not every connection is helping you—some are distractions, irrelevant to your goals, or cluttering your feed with low-value content.

Go to linkedin.com/mynetwork/ to review a list of your connections. To download your connections in a CSV file:

1. Go to LinkedIn home.
2. Click on "Me" in the top menu.
3. Select "Settings & Privacy."
4. In the left sidebar, click "Data Privacy."
5. Scroll down and select "Get a copy of your data."
6. Select "Download larger data . . ." options.
7. Click "Download archive." (It may take up to 48 hours to get your file.)

Organize and Clean Your LinkedIn Connections

It is infinitely easier to analyze and make decisions about your current connections once you put them into a spreadsheet. Once you get your CSV file from LinkedIn:

1. Import the CSV into a spreadsheet (Google Sheets or Excel) and format it for easy sorting and filtering. You may want to rename the columns to *Name, Job Title, Company, Connection Date*.
2. Insert a new column for "Category" and label each connection based on the following list:
   a. ICP Decision Makers & Influencers
   b. Existing Customer Contacts

    c. Professional Network

    d. Thought Leaders

    e. Internal Colleagues

    f. Low-Value Connections (irrelevant, spammy, or inactive connections that don't align with your objectives)

3. Remove your low-value connections. If you still wish to see their content in your feed, you can choose to follow them once you have removed the connection. If you're unsure about removing someone, check their recent activity. If they haven't posted or engaged in months, they likely aren't a valuable connection.

4. Sort the remaining connections by each category, identify gaps in your network, and develop a plan to connect with the people who should be in your network.

5. If you have access to a tool like ZoomInfo, use it to enhance your connections with contact information for fast prospecting outreach.

6. Add connections to your CRM as appropriate.

By cleaning up your existing connections and intentionally adding new strategic contacts, you'll transform your LinkedIn network into a more powerful sales tool.

This is an ongoing process. Your LinkedIn network is far more than a digital address book—it's a living, breathing ecosystem where business gets done. To maximize your return on network, we suggest auditing and refining your connections at least once a year or whenever you change sales roles or industries.

21

Always Be Connecting

Too many sellers treat networking like a temporary fix— something they do when the pipeline dries up, deals fall through, they get desperate, or a manager says, "You need to be more active on LinkedIn."

They send out a flurry of connection requests. But when their calendar fills back up, they go dark. The activity stops. The relationships go cold. And when they eventually circle back, they're starting from scratch. Reactive desperation never works.

Network building isn't a point in time, a box that you check, a one-and-done activity. It isn't something you do only when it is convenient. It is an infinite game.

To play the game at an elite level requires that you are intentional, aware, disciplined, and consistently focused on adding the right people to your network.

Opportunistic by Design

Top sales professionals look at every interaction—on- or offline—
and consider if it has the potential to expand their reach or open
new doors. When interacting with people, they ask themselves:

- Is this an ICP prospect and sales opportunity?
- Is this someone I can help?
- Is this someone who can help me?
- Is this someone I want to learn from or stay on the radar of?

Whether in sales conversations, at events and conferences,
while traveling, or even at church, school, and sports activities,
they're always looking for people who should be in their network.

They're opportunistic by design because they have done the
hard work to identify their ICP and know who should be in
their network. The highest earning sales professionals live by
the mantra *Always be connecting*.

Engineering Serendipity

Consider Brynne's connection with Jean, a fellow PTA mom.
Their bond started over something as simple as selling cupcakes
and attending kids' birthday parties. Sensing a mutual opportunity to help each other, Brynne connected with Jean on LinkedIn.

Years later, an announcement showed up in Brynne's
LinkedIn feed that Jean had taken a sales leadership role at
a company that was high on her target prospect list.

Brynne sent an LIDM to congratulate Jean, then called to
catch up. She invited Jean to one of her LinkedIn workshops as
a guest. This led to warm introductions to other leaders within
Jean's new company. A month later Brynne signed an agreement
to train the entire organization.

Then there's Beth from Jeb's team. Three years ago she sent a connection request to Aidan, who was a mid-level leader in one of her targeted ICP prospects. Over the years, she regularly interacted with Aidan's posts, and her posts showed up in his feed. From time to time he would comment on them, but he wasn't a decision-maker.

Last spring, Beth was walking through the airport when she heard someone shout her name. It was Aidan.

She stopped to say hello, excited to meet a digital connection in person. Aidan was excited to tell Beth that he'd been promoted to the head of his division and was glad to see her because he was hiring hundreds of salespeople and needed help training them on Sales Gravy methodologies. They agreed to meet the following week at his office in Dallas. A month later, Beth signed the largest contract of her entire career.

Both of these cases, and the thousands of other stories just like them, might seem like pure luck. But that could not be further from the truth. Luck has nothing to do with it.

Top performers engineer serendipity by doing the hard work of networking, connecting, and slow prospecting. They plant seeds by connecting thoughtfully, and over time allow small, intentional actions to compound into a powerful, self-sustaining stream of new opportunities.

You Reap What You Sow

Think of your network like a farmer considers their fields. In the winter, the farmer looks out over the empty fields and plans the crops. He decides what to grow, how much to grow, and when to harvest.

But if the farmer procrastinates, hesitates, doesn't follow through, and fails to sow the seeds, there will be no crops, no food for the family, and nothing to sell at the market, no matter the good intentions. The farmer who wants crops must take action to plant the seeds. In other words, he reaps what he sows.

Top sales professionals get this. They're always connecting. Planting seeds. Instead of waiting for the perfect opportunity, they take action to connect, follow up, and nurture their network until one connection becomes two, then 20, then 200.

The sellers who keep planting seeds even when they don't need immediate results are the ones who wake up one day with a network that feeds their pipeline.

- Don't wait for perfect timing—when you see an opportunity to connect, take it.

- View every interaction as an opportunity to grow your network. After every conversation, ask yourself, "Should I connect with this person on LinkedIn?" If the answer is yes, send a personalized connection request.

- Take advantage of familiarity peaks. Don't let good conversations go cold. Follow up while the interaction is still fresh. Consistent, thoughtful follow-up is what transforms casual connections into valuable relationships.

The right person, added at the right moment, can open doors that would've stayed locked for years. Always be connecting.

22

Sending Effective Connection Requests

One of the most frequent questions from participants in our LinkedIn Edge workshops is "How do I get people to accept my LinkedIn connections requests?"

When you send a connection request, no matter how much intention and thoughtfulness you put into it, there is always the chance that it may be rejected or ignored. No one likes sending a connection request into the void and getting ghosted or, worse, being outright rejected.

On the other hand, a well-crafted, personalized connection request improves the probability of acceptance and makes an important first impression. When done right, it opens the door to future pipeline opportunities, insightful conversations, warm introductions, referrals, and ultimately, new business.

Generic, Spammy, and Forgettable

On LinkedIn, you have the option of sending a standard, generic connection request, or you may customize and personalize your message. Here are three types of messages to avoid:

1. **Generic:** The generic request is fast and easy. Just click the connect button and hope. Since it's human nature to gravitate toward easy, most connection requests on LinkedIn are generic. And because generic doesn't stand out and people know you put little effort into it, the requests often get ignored.

2. **Spammy:** Self-serving sales pitches are a total turn-off and increase the likelihood that you get slammed with a hard rejection, blocked by that person, and reported to LinkedIn. Do enough of this and you may be permanently banned from the platform.

3. **Forgettable:** Meaningless messages like "I came across your profile and thought we should be connected because blah, blah, blah" are completely forgettable and likewise ignored. Do yourself a big favor and wipe the phrase "came across your profile" (or "came across [anything]") from your vocabulary forever. There may not be four more boring, meaningless, or lazy words. This phrase conveys that you've done no research and made no investment into getting to know the recipient.

Your connection request is the moment of truth in which you build a bridge to future, mutually beneficial opportunities. If you treat it like a checkbox—firing off generic requests, vague messages or, worse, sales pitches—you're burning potential relationships before they even start.

How to Write Effective Connection Request Messages That Get Accepted

The primary drivers that increase the likelihood that your connection request will be accepted are the recipient's familiarity with you, timing, and the quality, authenticity, and relevance of your message.

There are five key components of high-quality connection requests that make a great impression: Requests must be polite, professional, personalized, complimentary, and relevant. The good news is that when your message checks most or all of these five boxes, you're ahead of 90 percent of people in your recipient's inbox.

Polite

LinkedIn inboxes are flooded with impersonal pitches and generic connection requests. For this reason your polite, respectful approach immediately sets the right tone, differentiating and positioning you as someone worth connecting with.

Think of a LinkedIn connection request like a virtual handshake. Taking the time to be courteous, considerate, and clear isn't just about being nice—it's about building trust from the very first touchpoint.

Politeness signals professionalism, emotional intelligence, and respect—all of which increase the likelihood that your connection request will be accepted. And once that initial impression is formed, it becomes the foundation for future interactions.

When sending connection requests and follow-up messages, always follow the three Be's of Politeness:

- **Be respectful:** Give your recipient's position and experience the deference it deserves.
- **Be nice:** Approach with warmth and friendliness, avoiding pushy or aggressive language.

- **Be brief:** Respect the recipient's time. Get to the point without rambling or overloading your message.

Mastering these three elements keeps your connection request concise, considerate, and compelling.

Professional

First impressions are often formed in seconds. Grammar, punctuation, style, and the words you choose matter as much as how you dress for a meeting, show up on video, or speak on a sales call.

When you send a connection request, you're not just asking someone to add you to their network—you're giving them a glimpse of how you'll show up if they choose to engage with you.

- Is this person polished and credible?
- Are they intelligent?
- Do they understand business etiquette?
- Will they bring value to my network?
- Would I feel comfortable introducing them to other people in my network?

A professional, well-crafted connection request signals that you respect the recipient's time, space, and expertise. But a sloppy, overly casual, or tone-deaf message can derail the opportunity before it even begins.

Personalized

Treat every person you want to connect with like they have a sign on their profile picture that says, "Show me you know me," or "Make me feel important."

Do your research and get to know the person. Make your connection request message about them, not about you. When you take the time to personalize your message, you demonstrate that you care enough to do your homework and that you're genuinely interested in building a meaningful connection.

When someone sees that you've referenced a specific detail about their work, background, or interests, they immediately pay more attention. It activates the part of the brain that processes self-relevance. They feel seen, valued, and important—which makes them far more likely to accept your request.

Complimentary

Few things in human relationships are as powerful as a sincere, genuine compliment. When you tie your compliment to a specific achievement or insight, it shows that you've done your homework and are being genuine.

The key is to be specific and sincere. Generic, insincere praise like "Great profile!" or "Love your work!" (especially when AI generated) lands cold. No one wants to feel like they're being manipulated.

When done right, a well-placed compliment creates an immediate sense of goodwill and makes your connection request feel authentic rather than transactional.

Relevant

Rule number one for connection request acceptance is that people connect with you for their reasons, not yours. They want to know, "What's in it for me?"

This is why the biggest mistake sales professionals make is framing connection requests around their immediate agenda.

The goal of a connection request isn't to close a deal or hit a target or get something right now. It's about laying the foundation for a future opportunity. When you make your request about them—their work, their goals, their interests, their ego—you'll stand out, differentiate, and your connection request will be accepted.

Connection Request Messaging Templates

Writing connection requests should not be complicated. A little common sense and thoughtfulness go a long way. Here are a few connection request message ideas and templates to get you started.

Prior to an Event

> *[Name], I saw your post about attending the upcoming [event]. I'll also be there and am super excited. I'd love to catch up at the event and meet you in person! In the meantime, let's connect here on LinkedIn.*

> *[Name], I was reviewing the attendee list for [event] and was excited to see that you are on it. I've been following your posts here on LinkedIn for the past year and have learned a lot from you and your perspective on [subject, industry, technology]. Hopefully I'll have the chance to shake your hand while we're there. In the meantime, I hope you'll be open to connecting with me here on LinkedIn.*

Following an Event

> *[Name], I enjoyed meeting you at the [event, conference, trade show]. Your take on [subject, trend, idea etc.] was intriguing. I hope you enjoy [kids' soccer game, vacation, trip, hobby]. I look forward to staying connected and our next conversation.*

> *[Name], I saw that we both attended [event name] last month. The talks on [specific topic] were fantastic, right? I'd love to learn your perspective on [specific trend, topic, insight]. Let's connect."*

Following a Sales Call

[Name], Thank you for taking the time to meet with me today. I enjoyed learning about you and the challenges you're facing with [problem]. I look forward to our next meeting and sharing some ideas I have with you and your team. In the meantime, I noticed that we were not connected here on LinkedIn and thought I'd rectify that oversight on my part.

Following an Interaction

[Name], It was a pleasure meeting you on our flight to [city]. Thank you for your restaurant recommendations! Your take on [subject] really made me think differently about [subject]. I look forward to staying connected.

[Name], It was great to meet you this weekend at the [youth sporting event]. I hope you had a safe trip home. I was very impressed with your [son's, daughter's] performance. I look forward to staying connected with you.

Mutual Connection

[Name], I noticed that you are connected to my good friend [name] and since you are also [interested in, working in, located in, etc.] I thought it might make sense for us to be connected also.

[Name], My good friend and colleague [name] is connected with you and told me that you are the one person I absolutely must have in my network! Please accept my connection request.

[Name], I'm connected with your colleague(s) [name(s)] and thought it might make sense to connect with you as well since we are both in [industry].

Profile Visit

[Name], Thank you for visiting my profile. I had a chance to look at yours, and based on your interests, I think it might make sense for us to connect.

Connecting with Total Strangers

Very often, when attempting to connect with a multi-thread of stakeholders from a target prospect, you will be starting from scratch with familiarity. You don't know them. They don't know you.

Because you're in sales, they may be reluctant to accept your connection request. The most effective way to improve connection request acceptance in these cases is through systematically liking, commenting on, and sharing (LCS) their posts, along with commenting on their comments (positively) for a few weeks prior to sending your connection request. Then connect with a compliment:

[Name], I really appreciated your recent post on [topic]. Your insights on [key takeaway] gave me a fresh perspective—I'd love to stay connected and continue learning from your work.

[Name], I just listened to your conversation with [host] on the [podcast] about [specific topic]. It really resonated with me—so much so that I shared it with my entire team. I felt compelled to connect so that I can continue learning from you.

The LCS motion both builds familiarity and taps into the law of reciprocity. When you LCS someone's post, it is a gift of attention and makes them feel important. This increases the probability that they will accept your request because they are familiar with you and feel an obligation to return the favor.

Optimizing Connection Request Timing to Familiarity Peaks

A perfectly crafted connection request can still fall flat if the timing is wrong. Because familiarity increases connection request acceptance, your message should be sent as close to a familiarity peak as possible.

For example, let's say that, on a plane, you meet an executive from a company that matches your ICP. You have a nice discussion, exchange cards, and promise to "get together soon."

As you shake hands before disembarking, you've reached a familiarity peak. From that point forward, familiarity degrades and the clock is ticking on connection request acceptance.

Should you tuck the business card away and send a connection request a month later, acceptance probability plummets. But if you send a request that highlights your conversation the moment you get off the plane, your request will almost certainly be accepted.

This is why timing matters just as much as the quality of your messaging for compelling connection request acceptance.

Withdrawing a Connection Request

It is a good practice to monitor the status of your connection requests. When a request is still pending after 30 days with no response, it may make sense to withdraw it. To monitor or withdraw connection requests follow these steps:

- Go to "My Network" at the top of the LinkedIn page.
- Click "Show all" next to "Invitations."
- Switch to the "Sent" tab.
- Review and withdraw any stale or irrelevant requests.

When you withdraw a connection request on LinkedIn, the pending request disappears from the recipient's connection request inbox. They won't be notified that you withdrew the request, so if they haven't noticed the request in their queue, they'll never know you sent one.

Once you withdraw the request, you can try again with a new request after waiting 21 days. This gives you a second chance to make a stronger impression by crafting a more personalized, relevant message or investing in building familiarity and goodwill prior to your next attempt.

23

Avoid the Bait-and-Switch Connection Request

It is a very bad, no good, self-serving move to pitch someone as soon as they accept your connection request. You are not going to convert more prospects into customers by rewarding their goodwill with an immediate sledgehammer-to-the-forehead pitch.

(Here is an example from Jeb's inbox (Figure 23.1)).

"Thank you for connecting, now buy from me!" is a total turn-off that will result in your connection being rescinded, your message potentially reported as spam, and you being blocked.

None of us want to accept a connection request only to be immediately inundated by requests for favors, introductions, referrals, invitations to events, information gathering and qualifying, or inbound lead-gen tactics. When you rush in with a pitch before a connection is even interested in learning about you, you risk alienating them instead of attracting them.

Figure 23.1   Example of a bait-and-switch request.

Most people in a decision-making role have been burned like this after having accepted a connection request. It just feels "ugh!" because it sucks to be manipulated like this.

After a while these experiences add up and turn into suspicion and cynicism each time they get or accept a connection request. They are on the lookout for anything that proves their suspicion right. Until you lay a foundation of trust with consistent evidence that you are trustworthy, they will be suspicious of your motivations.

Build a Foundation of Trust One Brick at a Time

Rather than leading with your sales agenda, focus on building trust and goodwill. Invest time in nurturing and building familiarity.

Here is just one example of a trust-building, slow-prospecting sequence following a connection request acceptance:

Day 1: Send a kind follow-up note thanking them for connecting with you without any ask or request. Just a sincere thank you: *"[Name], Thank you very much for accepting my connection request. I look forward to following you and staying in touch."*

Day 3: Follow up with a like and comment on one of their posts.

Day 4: Repost one of their posts with your comment (sincere praise for their point of view goes a long way).

Day 7: Like and comment on another of their posts.

Day 9: Post a thoughtful and sincere comment on one of their posts that supports their position.

Day 10: Send a LinkedIn Direct Message (LIDM) complimenting them on one of the posts from day 9 (or anything else that makes sense).

Day 12: Share an appropriate post or job posting from their company page on your feed, to your audience and tag them in it.

Day 14: LIDM them an easy-to-consume article, resource, or LinkedIn post of interest that does not require them to fill out a form—no strings attached.

Day 15: Like, comment, and share one of their posts or comment on one of their comments.

Day 16: Write a post about the topic you discussed and quote or tag them in it.

Day 20: Send an LIDM and ask their opinion about something they will likely have an opinion on: one of their posts, a trend in their industry, an emerging idea or technology. The goal is to get them into a conversation. Do not pitch. If they lean in and engage, attempt to get them into a phone conversation so you really begin to build the relationship. *"[Name], absolutely loved your point of view on [reference subject or post]. I have a quick follow-up question, may I give you a call? [question]."*

Days 21–30: Continue to be consistent with a regular LCS routine.

Yes, we know, a 30-day process might sound tedious, but there's no shortcut to trust with a high-value stakeholder in a targeted ICP prospecting sequence. With slow prospecting on LinkedIn, patience is truly a virtue. There is no easy button.

Over the course of this sequence, you'll earn the right to ask for a favor, invite them to an event, share insights that support your sales agenda, offer resources that require them to complete a form, or ask for a meeting, qualifying information, and warm introductions.

When you build the foundation of trust slowly, one brick at a time, you reduce the probability that they will reject your request or remove the connection, while increasing the likelihood that they will engage and help you.

24

Rules and Best Practices for Accepting Connection Requests

A s your LinkedIn presence grows, so will your inbound connection requests—a good sign that your content, activity, and visibility are making an impact.

It's flattering when connection requests start pouring in. The temptation will always be there to accept every request that comes your way. But quantity isn't the goal—quality is. Treating your network like a vanity metric dilutes its strength and weakens your influence.

Many people, early in their LinkedIn journey, make the mistake of accepting every request that comes their way. Their network grows fast. It feels good at first, but soon they find that it's just noise—shallow connections that add no value, conversations that go nowhere.

Evaluate Each Invitation Carefully

You must be smart and vigilant about who you allow into your network. Every connection should serve a purpose. Before you click "accept," think twice. Ask yourself:

- Is this person's company aligned with my ICP?
- Do they fit the profile of the decision-makers and influencers I want in my network?
- Does this person have influence in my target industry or accounts?
- Could this connection lead to future introductions, insights, or referrals?
- Is there an obvious shared interest or common ground?
- Have they engaged with my content, referenced a mutual connection, or mentioned a relevant event?
- Are they likely to add value or amplify my network's reach?
- Will this connection help me grow my network strategically or add credibility to my profile?

If the answer is yes to any of these questions, accept the request and initiate a meaningful conversation.

It's Okay to Say No

For many people, declining (or simply not responding) to a connection request feels uncomfortable. There's unspoken pressure to accept every request because saying no can feel rude or like you are letting the other person down.

Another reason we sometimes struggle to decline requests is a sense of obligation. We're wired to reciprocate when someone shows interest in us. When a connection request comes in— especially from someone who seems eager to connect—there's a natural impulse to say yes out of politeness.

It's also easy to worry that you might miss an opportunity because you didn't connect. This fear keeps you stuck in reactive mode, saying yes to every request out of anxiety that one missed connection could cost you down the line.

Allowing a new connection into your network for the wrong reasons doesn't serve anyone. It doesn't create value for you or for them.

The fact is that a weak, unaligned LinkedIn connection is just as ineffective as no connection at all. So, it's okay to say no. Curating your network with intention is a form of self-respect and strategic discipline. Accepting the wrong connections dilutes your network and clutters your feed with worthless noise.

Ask for Clarification

If you are still unsure if someone is a fit, it's also okay to ask for clarification and more information before making a decision:

> *[Name], Thanks for the invite to connect. Typically, I connect with people I either know or have had engagement with here on LinkedIn or in other venues. May I ask how you found me and what triggered the connection request?*

Be selective. Saying no to the wrong connections allows you to say a more powerful yes to the right ones.

Engage in Conversations with Inbound Connections

With inbound connection requests, it is right and proper to engage in a conversation to quickly learn how you can help them, and they can help you.

Immediately after accepting, send a thank you message and ask a question related to the sender's message, profile, or interests. The objective is to initiate and engage in a dialogue. Here are examples:

> *[Name], Thanks for adding me to your network. I noticed you are a [title] at [company] and would like to learn more about your business. I'm curious, [ask an open-ended question].*

> *[Name], Thanks for connecting! I noticed you're focused on [specific initiative or trend]. How are you approaching [related challenge]?"*

> *[Name], Thanks for adding me to your network. I saw that you recently transitioned into a new role at [company name]. Congratulations! How's the transition been going for you?"*

> *[Name], Thanks for adding me to your network. I noticed from your posts that you attended the [conference] in [city] last month. I was there too. What was your favorite session?*

Typically, when someone is asking you to connect, there is a reason. Getting them to engage in a conversation is the surest and fastest way to initiate a relationship and bring that reason to the surface. Very often this leads to an immediate, mutually beneficial business opportunity.

Build a Network That Works for You

The beauty of LinkedIn is that your network is what you make it. By being intentional, strategic, and thoughtful about who you allow into your circle, you're curating a network that creates opportunities—one that amplifies your visibility, deepens your credibility, and opens doors that would otherwise remain closed.

25

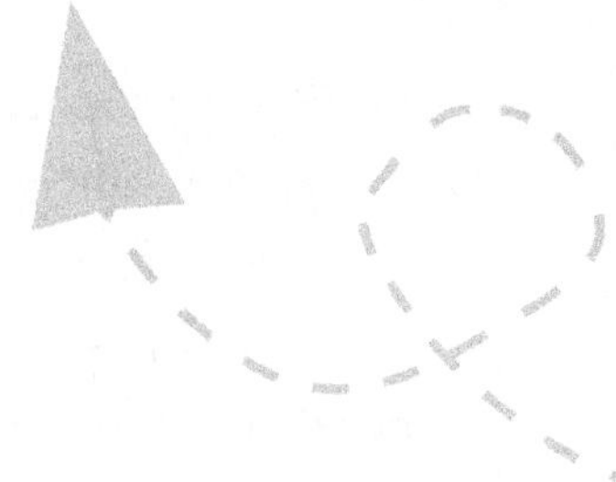

Nurture Your Network

Nurturing your network is just as important as building it. But far too often, sales professionals put all of their attention on building (planting seeds) and very little on nurturing and cultivating. As Brynne likes to say, they "connect and forget."

Once you've established connections, the real work begins. The entire point of building your network is to make it productive so that you generate more pipeline opportunities and ultimately sell more.

This doesn't happen in a vacuum. You cannot connect and forget. You must invest in daily activities to make the magic happen. These slow prospecting activities include:

- Staying visible and top of mind
- Building your personal brand as a valued content and insight contributor
- Strengthening and anchoring relationships through interaction and conversation

- Being a connector who brings people together for mutual benefit
- Leveraging the Law of Reciprocity by giving value.

Tending to your network consistently keeps you visible and your network viable. This is exactly why you must schedule regular time blocks each day for investing in your network.

Much of our discussion going forward in this book will be focused on executing these strategies effectively to harvest tangible sales outcomes from your network building and slow prospecting activity.

The Law of Reciprocity

Robert Cialdini, the author of *Influence*, explains, "One of the most potent of the weapons of influence around us is the rule for reciprocation. The rule says that we should try to repay, in kind, what another person has provided us."

When you give something of value—attention, appreciation, insight, or assistance—you create a subtle but powerful sense of obligation. In other words, when you give value first, your connections have a tendency to respond in kind.

Whether it's agreeing to an appointment, considering your offer, making an introduction, accepting your connection request, committing to a next step, or giving you a referral, the compelling desire to balance the scales nudges them to give back to you.

Play the Long Game and Be Consistent

The key to leveraging the law of reciprocity is consistency. Don't expect one act of giving to generate immediate results. Play the long game. Keep showing up. Keep giving. Keep acknowledging and supporting your connections.

People will notice. They appreciate you when you give without being asked. They respect you when you go the extra mile. They remember you when you make them feel important.

The favor will be returned. You create a flywheel of goodwill that eventually pays off with leads, new pipeline opportunities, introductions, and referrals. Play the long game. Build trust. Give more than you take. The law of reciprocity will do the rest.

Lead with Value

When you lead with value, prospects stop seeing you as just another salesperson chasing a quota and start viewing you as a trusted resource and partner. This shift in perception is powerful.

The good news is that this approach is very simple. It's primarily about being nice: offering small gestures of kindness that make people feel important, and being thoughtful about helping others out.

It doesn't mean overwhelming prospects with endless articles, resources, white papers, or unsolicited advice. It doesn't mean peppering them with incessant, contrived questions to get their "opinion" or "thoughts."

The key is being authentically human and *other-focused*. You must be aware, strategic, and intentional. It's putting your empathy to work understanding what matters to your prospect, then offering something to them that's timely, relevant, and genuinely helpful.

Make Me Feel Important

Mary Kay Ash, founder of Mary Kay cosmetics, said that you should "Pretend that every single person you meet has a sign around their neck that says, 'Make me feel important.' Not only will you succeed in sales, you will succeed in life."

The most insatiable human need is to feel important, that we matter. It is the singularity of human behavior in the first world.

In conversations with other people, humans spend as much as 60 percent of the time talking about themselves. Move those conversations to LinkedIn and the number reaches 80 percent or higher. We're all seeking attention to fill the unfillable need for significance.

This, by the way, is why we feel so emotionally connected to people who listen to us and disconnected from people who talk at us. When you lean in, give attention to and make someone feel important, you give them the greatest gift you can give another human being, thus sparking a powerful desire in that person to reciprocate.

A Systematic Approach to Making People Feel Important

The most effective sales professionals on LinkedIn aren't just scrolling aimlessly and doing random acts of kindness. They are systematic in their approach to spotting key moments that create natural openings to make others feel important.

Catch-Up Feature

One of the easiest ways to monitor your network is using the Catch-up feature on the LinkedIn network tab. This feature clues you into job changes, birthdays, work anniversaries, and education changes—all opportunities for a kind note of congratulations and a compliment.

To access this feature:

1. Go to the LinkedIn home page.
2. Click on the "My Network" tab in the top menu.
3. Click on the "Catch up" tab in the network window in Figure 25.1.

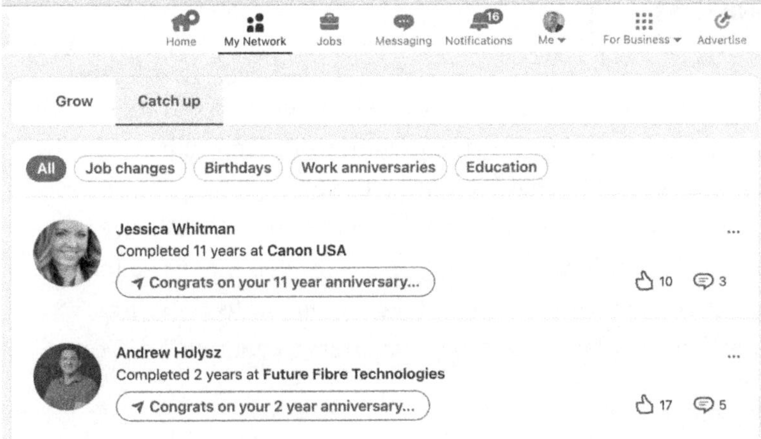

Figure 25.1   LinkedIn Network Catch-up feature.

Sales Navigator Alerts

Sales Navigator *alerts* give you a front row seat to your prospect's behavior—surfacing opportunities to make prospects feel important, spark conversations, and trigger reciprocity, including:

- Posts, shares, and comments so you can engage at the right moments
- Promotions, awards, work anniversaries, and achievements where a genuine compliment can make them feel seen and appreciated
- Job changes where a sincere "Congratulations!" can make your prospect's day

Most salespeople only scratch the surface with these alerts, but there is so much you can do in Navigator to keep abreast of your network.

Give Likes

The easiest way to spark reciprocity is by engaging with your prospect's content. On LinkedIn, where most people are shouting for attention, those who give attention—thoughtfully, sincerely, and consistently—stand out like a beacon.

Most people look at their posts and count the likes (reactions). Those likes are a vanity measure that many use to measure their self-worth. So take a moment to click "like," "love," or "applause," because it matters to your connections.

Comment

But don't just click "like" and move on. The real gift is commenting on their posts. Comments signal that you cared enough to actually read their post, that you value them and their opinion. Comments also drive the LinkedIn algorithm, giving their post more visibility.

The key to effective commenting is sincerity. Avoid being cheesy, gratuitous, or engaging in any self-promotion.

- Sometimes this means that the best comment is a simple: "This is awesome!" or "Love this!" or something similar.
- At other times, especially with deep content, it makes more sense to write a thoughtful comment that supports their position or adds to the conversation without stealing their thunder.
- In cases where you notice that the author of the post is super active and responsive in comments, you might attempt to engage in a conversation by asking a question after your comment. Just be careful that your question is relevant and will be appreciated.

If you are searching for an appropriate comment but can't seem to find the right words, you can always tap into AI for help.

The best thing about leaving comments is that they make you memorable. Your connection may not see your face and name when you like their post, but they will see you when you comment. This moves you closer to the familiarity threshold.

Share Their Content

Sharing takes commenting to the next level. When you repost their post to your feed and share it with your audience, it is a powerful compliment.

Don't just click "Repost." *Always* choose "Repost with your thoughts."

- In a hurry, you can repost with a simple "Love this inspirational post from [tag them]. It's a must read."
- It's even better when your thoughts are deeper and provide additional value and insights. Here is an example:

Jeb Blount nailed it with his Money Monday podcast about George Foreman's legendary ability to pivot, adapt, and come back stronger. His journey from heavyweight champion to global brand icon is a testament to the power of resilience—a quality that separates top-performing sales professionals from the pack.

In sales, resilience means:

- *Staying consistent with prospecting even when responses are sparse*
- *Reframing rejection as part of the process, not a reflection of your worth*
- *Having the mental toughness to keep pushing forward when most would give up*

Jeb's post is a timely reminder that, like Foreman, the best sales pros stay in the fight long after others have thrown in the towel.

What's one way you build mental resilience in your sales process?

#Resilience #SalesDiscipline #Persistence #NeverGiveUp

Reposting with your thoughts does two things: First, it allows you to curate their content on your feed. Most importantly, it gives you an opportunity to publicly compliment and support them. This is another place where AI can give you a hand with crafting your message. Just be sure to edit and humanize what AI gives you.

AI PRO TIP

Repost Prompt: I want to repost this LinkedIn post from [name] with my thoughts. I need my message to be complimentary of [name] and provide additional value and insights to their post. Here is their original post: [paste here].

Give Genuine Compliments

Abraham Lincoln once said, "Everyone likes a compliment." You should never miss an opportunity to compliment someone in public and privately. Nothing is more powerful. On LinkedIn those opportunities abound:

- Post your congratulations and compliments publicly on job change announcements, achievements, certifications, and milestones.
- Create new posts (when appropriate) that compliment something your network connection has done or achieved—tag their boss and peers for maximum impact.
- Send private LIDM or InMail messages, video messages, and voice messages to compliment them.

When people feel approved of and valued, you boost their self-esteem. They like themselves more, and because of this, they like you more.

Say Thank You

Few things are as powerful in human relationships as a simple thank you. Showing gratitude toward someone doesn't need to be saved for a special occasion. Take a moment to say thank you when:

- A connection request is accepted.
- Someone visits your profile.
- People comment on or share your post.
- Your connection posts particularly insightful, interesting, or inspiring content.
- After every meeting or conversation.
- People endorse you or give you recommendations.

- You get warm introductions and referrals.
- Someone compliments you.

As Sterling Brown said, "Always have an attitude of gratitude," because everyone appreciates a thank you.

Share Valuable Resources

While monitoring the posts and comments of your network connections, you'll often notice that they are working through problems. Under the right circumstances, this opens the door to help them out with valuable resources that you have or know about that they don't.

Valuable is the key word here. This does not mean sending them a resource that requires them to leap through a lead-gen form, or wade through one of your marketing brochures, or sift through self-promoting blogs or videos.

For this effort to pay off, the value and ideas you give must be:

- Specific to their problem
- Timely
- Something that can actually help them
- Free from blatant self-promotion

This is an example of a simple LIDM message for this type of resource:

I noticed from your recent posts that you're dealing with [specific problem]. I've attached a link to [resource] that one of my clients said helped them with a similar challenge. I hope you find this useful, too.

This genuine, low-key approach positions you as a trusted resource and opens the door for both reciprocity and a future conversation.

Endorse Skills

Endorsements are an easy, low-effort way to acknowledge a connection's expertise and stay top of mind with a small but meaningful gesture. All it takes is a few seconds and a simple click of a button next to a skill on their profile in the Skills & Endorsements section.

For maximum visibility and to ensure that they notice your gesture, you may choose to follow up with an LIDM note like this:

> *[Name], I just endorsed you for [skill or expertise] because I've seen firsthand the value you bring in that area. I'd be happy to provide a more detailed recommendation if that would be helpful.*

When you endorse a connection for a particular skill, it adds credibility to their profile by showing that you and others vouch for their competence and experience, which boosts their authority and influence.

Write Thoughtful Recommendations

Writing LinkedIn Recommendations is an uber-powerful reciprocity tool that will absolutely strengthen your professional relationships and get attention. Recommendations carry emotional weight and create a strong sense of obligation for the recipient to reciprocate.

Thoughtfulness is the key. This isn't something you do on a whim. Your recommendation must be authentic, specific, earned, and highlight specific contributions, achievements, tangible results or qualities that made an impact. It should mention your relationship, the context of your work together, and why you're recommending them.

To write a recommendation, simply go to the "Recommendations" section of your connection's profile and click the "Recommend [name]" button.

Here is an example:

I had the pleasure of collaborating with [Name] on [specific project or initiative], and their expertise in [industry or skill] was invaluable. Their ability to [specific contribution] not only [achieved a particular result] but also demonstrated exceptional [trait (e.g., leadership and strategic thinking)]. I highly recommend [Name] for anyone looking to work with a true professional who brings tremendous value to the table.

As a reciprocity tool, a recommendation is the gift that keeps on giving because it remains on your connection's profile indefinitely, reinforcing your gesture of kindness and always reminding them of you.

Connector Currency

Making introductions and referrals and connecting people in your network is among the highest forms of value. When the connections you make turn into valuable business relationships, reciprocity is almost always right around the corner.

People who benefit from your introductions become advocates for your work and naturally want to reciprocate by referring opportunities your way. In the long game of slow prospecting, being known as someone who brings people together is an unmatched competitive advantage.

There are so many ways on LinkedIn to give your connections the gift of importance. Use these strategies to create a powerful reciprocity loop that generates leads, meetings, conversations, introductions, and referrals.

26

Multi-threading

Imagine walking into a networking event at your local chamber of commerce. Do you only talk to the first person you meet and call it a night? No, that wouldn't make any sense. Instead, you mingle, you chat with multiple folks, sharing stories and making connections.

That's multi-threaded network building in a nutshell. It's about putting your eggs in multiple baskets, so that you avoid getting single siloed with one stakeholder within a targeted account.

Multi-threading is about having conversations with multiple stakeholders simultaneously and going high, wide, and deep within an account. This allows you to build a more comprehensive understanding of the organization, its needs, and the various influencers involved in the buying decision.

The Benefits of Multi-threading

In the complex dance of B2B sales, decisions aren't made in isolation. These days, on average, there are typically 11 or more stakeholders involved in important buying decisions.

This is why you must actively work to identify and talk with each person who has a "stake" in the outcome of the deal, diversifying your outreach across different contacts within an organization. By engaging multiple stakeholders, you're amplifying your chances of hitting the right note that gets the deal moving while de-risking your position on the sales chessboard.

- Focus fast prospecting sequences on multiple stakeholders to give yourself more opportunities to open the door.

- Leverage slow prospecting strategies to connect and build relationships with multiple people within a targeted organization to gain warm introductions to economic decision-makers, gather qualifying information, cultivate future buying windows, and gain insight into pain points, problems, and organizational aspirations.

- Reduce the risk of losing active pipeline deals by widening your relationships and visibility across the stakeholder map and collaborating with them on solution development as you progress through the steps of the sales process.

- Improve your win probability by building a coalition for stakeholders who advocate for you and your business case, reducing obstacles and objections.

EXERCISE 26.1 LINK JOB TITLES TO BUYING ROLE PERSONAS

The starting point for mapping stakeholders is identifying your ideal customer persona (ICP) buying group: Who are the key players? Who has a stake? Who has influence beyond those in a traditional decision-maker role?

1. Start by going back to Chapter 2 and reviewing your
   answers from the ICP analysis questions.
2. Make a list of the various job titles of the people within
   your targeted ICP prospects who make buying decisions,
   influence buying decisions, and use or are impacted by
   your product, service, or software.
3. Make a list of the nomenclature variations for each job
   title or role you have identified (this is a perfect job to
   hand off to your AI).
4. Next link these titles to the key personas in the buying
   process: Decision-Makers, Influencers, Users,
   or Coaches.

ICP Buying Group Job Titles	Job Title Variations	Buying Role Personas: Decision-Maker, Influencer, User, Coach

EXERCISE 26.2 IDENTIFY AND MAP STAKEHOLDERS

The next challenge is finding the actual names of these key
stakeholders within your target prospects and accounts.
The good news is that LinkedIn and other tools have made
this process much easier.

(Continued)

(*Continued*)

CRM Search

Begin with searching your CRM for contacts from the same company and determine if any of them match your ICP buying group job titles. The AI built into your CRM may be able to speed this process up for you.

Website Review

Search your target prospect's website for key contacts. You'll often find the profiles of top leaders listed on the website. AI can speed this process up for you. See the following prompt in the AI Pro Tip.

AI PRO TIP

Website Search Prompt: Please review this website [website URL]. I want you to search for people from this company with the titles: [list titles, comma separated]. Please put your findings into table format that includes the person's name, title, email, phone, and link to the page where you found the information.

LinkedIn Company Page

Go to your target prospect's LinkedIn Company Page. Click the "people" tab. Scroll down and you'll find a list of employees. Going through the list of employees can be a time-consuming process with large organizations with many employees, but it's a good place to start. The good news is that AI can do this work for you in a flash, and once you have the list, use ZoomInfo to get contact information.

Sales Data Tools

ZoomInfo, Apollo, and Seamless have rich data and powerful AI-powered search functions that can quickly help you drill down and identify the individuals and contact information for the members of your target prospect's buying group.

We're big fans of ZoomInfo's org chart feature that gives you a visual hierarchy within your target company. This makes it even easier to identify relevant individuals who should be included in your multi-thread.

LinkedIn Profile and Post Review

Go to your primary contact's LinkedIn profile. Scroll down to the "people you may know from (name) company" widget on the right-hand side of their profile to find other people who might be relevant for your multi-thread. Check their activity and posts. People will often engage with or mention colleagues with whom they work closely and are often involved in buying decisions.

LinkedIn FREE Basic Search

To use filters to identify people for your multi-thread:

1. Click on the search bar, leave it blank, and hit return/enter.
2. Click on "All filters."
3. In the "Filter only" section, make sure the drop-down is on "People."
4. Scroll down to "Current Company" and type in the company name.
5. Scroll down to keywords and add all the titles in your buying committee.

For a Boolean search, enter a basic string like ("Job Title") AND ("Company Name") into the search bar.

You can get even more precise with a string like (HR OR "Human Resources") AND ("Director" OR "Vice President").

This will return a list of people with your desired job title who are currently working at the specified company.

LinkedIn Sales Navigator

To search for key buying roles at your target prospect and save a list:

1. Go to Sales Navigator.
2. Click on "Lead Search."
3. Apply filters:

   Company Name (e.g., Target Account)
   Department (e.g., IT, Sales, Operations, Finance)
   Seniority Level (e.g., Director, VP, C-Level)
   Keywords (e.g., "procurement," "budget," "evaluation")
   Spotlights (e.g., "Changed Jobs in the Past 90 Days" for new stakeholders)

4. Save relevant profiles to a "Buying Committee" list for tracking and outreach.

Boolean search in Sales Navigator is primarily needed if you are looking for keywords that will appear in their profile, but are not in their title.

Their title may be Director of HR, but you might want specific job descriptions to home in on the right Director of HR. In this case, you can click on the "Search Keywords" search bar on the top of your search results and add a search like (benefits OR healthcare) NOT (talent or recruiting).

You may also use this Boolean search string: ("IT Director" OR "VP of IT" OR "Head of Security") AND "Target Company Name".

Relationship Explorer

The Relationship Explorer in Sales Navigator can significantly enhance your ability to navigate complex multi-threads and establish valuable connections.

Lead Recommendations

The Relationship Explorer utilizes your defined target persona and seniority level to generate a curated list of top contacts within specific companies. This list prioritizes individuals who match your ideal customer profile. This helps you target prospects who are likely to be interested in your offerings.

The LinkedIn Relationship Map and ZoomInfo Org Chart: A Strategic Duo for Navigating Complex Accounts

The LinkedIn Relationship Map offers a dynamic, visual layout of the connections among individuals within a target account, helping you understand how people are networked together inside an organization.

This map becomes a powerful tool for identifying decision-makers, influencers, and other potential members of your targeted buying group—not just by their titles, but by how they are connected to each other and to you.

This helps you uncover who knows whom, who regularly engages with each other's content, and where there may be relationship bridges you can cross to warm up your outreach.

But while LinkedIn gives you a relationship lens, it doesn't always show the full organizational picture. That's where ZoomInfo's Org Chart feature becomes the perfect complement.

ZoomInfo's Org Chart provides a hierarchical view of the company structure, organized by department and role. It shows reporting relationships, seniority levels, and job functions, giving you the internal architecture behind the faces you see on LinkedIn.

Comparing LinkedIn's Relationship Map with ZoomInfo's Org Chart gives you a 360-degree view of the account: who matters, who influences whom, who reports to whom, and who might open the door to someone else. This insight enables you to approach multi-threading with surgical precision.

By taking time to study the social and structural connections inside your target accounts, you set the stage for using those insights to develop relationships with the right people early in the process. Rather than reaching out blindly and then talking your way in, you read the room before they ever enter it.

27

Making the Shift from Cold Calls to Warm Introductions

Imagine you're at a packed industry conference. You scan the room and spot a prospect you've been trying to connect with for months. You could march over, interrupt them, and launch into your pitch. But they don't know you, they don't trust you, and they're probably not in the mood for an unsolicited sales conversation. The odds are stacked against you that they lean in, pay attention, and respond positively.

Now imagine a different scenario. You're standing with a friend, colleague, customer, vendor, sales professional from a different industry, or an advisor (consultant, lawyer, accountant, banker, wealth manager) who knows your prospect personally. They wave them over and introduce you by saying, "Hey, you need to meet [your name]. They're doing some incredible work in your space. I think you two would hit it off."

That warm introduction and referral changes everything. The prospect is now curious, open, and far more likely to engage. You leverage the other person's familiarity and trust to instantly cross your prospect's familiarity threshold with little effort.

This is the essence of *social proximity*—the concept that the closer you are to someone through mutual connections, the higher your credibility and the lower the resistance. On LinkedIn, social proximity is one of the most powerful tools you have for pipeline building and closing.

Social Proximity at Work

Michael, a seasoned enterprise account executive, had been circling a $4 billion company for weeks. It was the kind of account every rep dreams of—high visibility, complex challenges, and a massive budget.

His solution was tailor-made for the company's financial management infrastructure. He knew that the chief financial officer (CFO) was the key decision-maker. But after running a multi-touch fast-prospecting sequence, he couldn't get the CFO to bite.

Inboxes at that level are a fortress and gatekeepers impenetrable. Michael's emails were opened, but never replied to. His InMails went unread. His calls were intercepted by an unyielding gatekeeper or went straight to the CFO's voicemail that was always full.

Nothing was working. Michael knew it was time to deploy a different strategy.

Work the Edges to Get to the Center

Michael turned to LinkedIn Sales Navigator and started building out a visual map of the company's leadership structure.

As he analyzed the potential buying committee, he spotted something interesting. The VP of finance and strategy, an executive named Chandra Gupta, who was one layer down from the CFO, showed up in his extended network—a second-degree connection.

Digging deeper, he realized this VP had significant influence over financial planning and business strategy—not the final say for an enterprise-level solution like Michael's, but definitely an influential voice the CFO listened to.

The magic happened when Michael discovered that he shared a first-degree connection to Chandra with Margret Lindell, a colleague who he'd worked with years earlier at a previous company.

Playing the Slow Game to Build Familiarity

Rather than rushing to ask Margret for a warm introduction, Michael started engaging with Chandra's content on LinkedIn. He added thoughtful, relevant comments and occasionally shared those posts with his own network—adding his perspective on governmental and regulatory challenges that impacted long-term financial strategy planning and compliance in Chandra's industry. Several times Chandra responded to his comments and visited Michael's profile.

The Warm Introduction

Sensing the time was right, he made two important moves. First he sent Chandra a personalized connection request:

> *Chandra, I've enjoyed reading your posts. Your take on strategic planning and how AI will be impacting corporate financial management in the coming years is insightful and way ahead of the rest of the industry. I hope you'll accept my connection request.*

Next he asked Margret for a warm introduction:

> *Margret, congratulations on your recent promotion. It's been so much fun watching your success! I noticed you're connected with Chandra over at Imtech. I've been following his impressive work and thought leadership. I have a strategic planning solution that can help his team. Would you be willing to introduce us?*

Margret responded immediately. Not only did she make the introduction—she personally vouched for Michael, framing him as an expert, friend, and someone she trusted.

Persistence and Proximity: A Powerful Combination

That one introduction shifted the entire trajectory of the opportunity. Within days, Michael had his first meeting with Chandra and a week later was on a discovery call with the CFO. Nine months later, he closed the biggest deal of his career. All thanks to social proximity and a little slow prospecting ingenuity.

Too many sellers go straight to the top, and when the door doesn't open, they give up. Michael's story is a masterclass in persistence and using social proximity to reach his target. When chasing the decision-maker failed, rather than giving up, he worked the edges and earned his way to the center of the buying committee.

Why Warm Introductions Work

Warm introductions are more than just polite gestures. They work because they tap into one of the most powerful forces in human psychology: *social proof.*

When someone we trust recommends a person or product, we're naturally more inclined to listen. On LinkedIn, this plays out in three key ways:

1. **Familiarity and credibility transfer:** The trust your mutual connection has with the prospect is extended to you. This removes skepticism and opens the door for a meaningful conversation.

2. **Differentiation:** Decision-makers are flooded with unsolicited messages. A warm introduction cuts through all of this and gets your foot in the door.

3. **Lower resistance:** People are more receptive to conversations that originate from trusted sources. This neutralizes common objections to first-time appointments, advancing to next steps, and closing the sale.

Before LinkedIn

Brynne was early in her sales career the first time she met Paul. He was a longtime customer of her company—old-school, successful, and respected in his industry. Her boss had handed her Paul's account earlier that week.

The meeting had gone well. They hit it off as if they were old friends. As they wrapped up, Brynne leaned in and asked the question every smart salesperson asks: "Paul, is there anyone else in your network you think I should be talking to?"

Before LinkedIn, there was the Rolodex—a spinning wheel of business cards and handwritten notes that sat on every executive's desk like a trophy. It wasn't just a contact list—it was a symbol of status, grit, and hustle. "How big is your Rolodex?" was the question of the day.

Without saying a word, Paul turned in his chair and reached over to the massive Rolodex sitting on the corner of his desk. It was well-worn, heavy, stuffed with decades of contacts and notes.

He spun it slowly, scanning the cards like a DJ searching for the perfect track. Then, with a flick of the wrist, he pulled out a single card. He scribbled a name and number from the card on a sticky note and handed it to Brynne. "Call her," he said. "Tell her I sent you."

Brynne nodded, grateful. Then she had a realization. *If I had access to that entire Rolodex—even for just one hour—it would change everything.* That moment was the catalyst that led her to eventually realize the true power of LinkedIn.

A New Level Playing Field

Paul's Rolodex wasn't just a list of contacts. It was a curated map of trust—a private network built one conversation, one handshake, one relationship at a time. But back then, those networks were locked down. Guarded. Protected. Shared sparingly, and only with those who had earned their way into the sanctum.

Fast-forward to today, LinkedIn has leveled the playing field. It's taken what was once hidden behind a fortress and made it accessible to everyone. Every connection you make unlocks a window into their network—who they know, who they engage with, and how you might earn your way in.

Unlike the days of the physical Rolodex, you don't have to sit and hope for a name to be handed over. With a few clicks, you can map entire buying committees, identify warm paths to decision-makers, and see how you're socially connected to the people you want to meet most.

The game of getting warm introductions and referrals hasn't changed—you still need to build relationships, earn the right, and ask—but the tools have. And for those who know how to use them, the opportunities are endless.

28

Social Proximity and the Best Path In

The most strategic use of your LinkedIn network is to create warm paths to reaching your ideal prospects through social proximity. Instead of relying only on cold outreach, you're leveraging existing connections to gain access and credibility.

Most often, you will be seeking warm introductions to *second-degree* connections. These are people connected to your first-degree connections but not directly to you.

First-degree connections have a direct line of communication and, presumably, a level of familiarity with your second-degree target. Your mutual first-degree connection can facilitate introductions, vouch for your credibility, or provide valuable access into your targeted ICP prospects. This makes a warm introduction more likely to be accepted.

To see how your LinkedIn connections are connected to other people, you can use a few built-in LinkedIn tools and features.

Look at Mutual Connections on Their Profile

When you visit someone's profile, LinkedIn will often display a list of mutual connections under their headline or in a dedicated section labeled "People You Both Know." Click the number of mutual connections to see the list. From there, identify someone you know well who could potentially make a warm introduction.

Use LinkedIn Search and Filters

If you're targeting a company or specific person, you can reverse-engineer how you're connected:

1. In the Search bar, type the company name or the person's name.

2. Click "People" > use the "Connections" filter.

3. Choose second-degree connections to surface people you're not connected to, but who are connected to someone you know.

This helps you see the pathways between you and your target.

Use the "Connections" Tab on Your Mutual Contact's Profile

If you're already connected to someone and want to see if they know someone you're targeting:

1. Go to your connection's profile.

2. Click on their "Connections" (if visible—they must have this setting enabled).

3. Search within their connections using keywords like the company name, title, or individual name.

This is useful for identifying bridges between your existing network and your target accounts.

Boolean Strings

When targeting specific types of connections, you can use Boolean searches like *"VP of Sales" AND "Acme Corp"* in the People Search bar. Then filter to second-degree connections to see if you have a mutual path.

Sales Navigator's Relationship Mapping

Sales Navigator offers a powerful tool for identifying social proximity through its relationship mapping feature:

1. Search for your target account and navigate to the company page inside Sales Navigator.
2. Click on the "People" tab to view employees.
3. Use the "Relationship" filter to find second-degree connections inside the organization.
4. Sales Navigator will show how you are connected (who your mutual first-degree contact is) and their job title.

You can then message your mutual connection directly from Sales Navigator and request a warm introduction.

"Best Path In" on Sales Navigator

Best Path In highlights social proximity pathways. It is a dynamic feature in Sales Navigator that surfaces your strongest mutual connections to a specific contact at a target company. It uses relationship strength and mutual activity signals to suggest who is most likely to help you get a warm introduction.

1. In Sales Navigator, search for the person (lead) you want to connect with.

2. Once you're on their Sales Navigator profile, look for the "Best Path In" section—usually located on the right side of the screen or under the Relationship tab.

3. Review suggested paths and first-degree mutual connections who could introduce you.

The GEAR Introduction Request Framework

Not all introduction requests are created equal. If you approach it the wrong way, you risk making your connection feel used or uncomfortable. The goal is to make it easy for them to say yes and help you.

Vague requests like "Can you introduce me to someone at XYZ Company?" rarely work. Instead follow the GEAR framework:

1. **Greet** them politely and identify the specific person you want to meet.

2. **Explain** why you want the introduction and why it makes sense for both parties.

3. **Ask** directly for the introduction and offer to write the intro for them.

4. **Remove** the pressure and be gracious for their consideration.

Here's an example:

Regina,

It was so nice to see you at the Emerging Tech Conference last month! I noticed you're connected to Jesse Argile, the founder of XAgent.ai. I've been following what they're building with their AI agent platform—it's impressive and right in our lane.

We specialize in fractional CFO services for scaling tech start-ups, and I saw that they're actively looking for a CFO. Based on what we do and who we serve, I think there's a real opportunity to help them get the talent they need to scale up fast.

Would you be open to making a warm introduction? I'm happy to send a short blurb that you can just forward if that makes it easier on you.

No pressure at all if it's not a fit or the timing's off—I just thought it might be worth a quick connection.

Appreciate you either way,

Felix Matteo

AI PRO TIP

AI can give you a hand with writing introduction requests. Use this prompt:

I need help writing a request to a LinkedIn first-degree connection for an introduction to one of their second-degree connections. I want my request message to follow the GEAR framework: Greet them politely. Explain why I want the introduction. Ask directly for the introduction and offer to write it for them. Remove the pressure and be grateful for the consideration. The name of my first-degree connection is [name]. The name of their second-degree connections is [name]. The second-degree connection is [title, role, function, specialty] at [company]. This target person is currently [searching for, dealing with, struggling with this specific challenge]. My company [your company name] provides [your solution] to [ICP] and this company is a perfect fit for what we do.

Introduction Blurb Template

Should your first-degree connection respond, asking for a short blurb, use this template:

I would like to introduce you to [your full name] from [your company]. [Your first name] has been instrumental in helping [companies or people] with [specific services or solutions you provide]. While I understand that [specific field or service] might not be a focus for you at the moment, I believe a conversation with [your first name] could be advantageous. [He/she/they] will be reaching out soon, but feel free to contact [your first name] directly at [your contact information].

Following Up After an Introduction

Once your first-degree connection has made the introduction, it's your responsibility to keep the momentum going. Respond promptly and professionally. Express appreciation to both the introducer and the prospect. After the conversation, follow up with your connection to let them know how it went.

[Name], Thank you so much for the introduction to [prospect's name]. We had a great conversation, and I really appreciate your help in making it happen. Please let me know how I can return the favor!

You can take your gratitude up a notch with a handwritten thank you note and small gift of appreciation.

A Powerful Interconnected Ecosystem

When you understand and apply the concept of social proximity, your LinkedIn network becomes a powerful ecosystem that accelerates trust, opens doors that would otherwise stay closed, and generates meaningful sales conversations.

PART 4

Personal Branding and the LinkedIn Profile Lead Machine

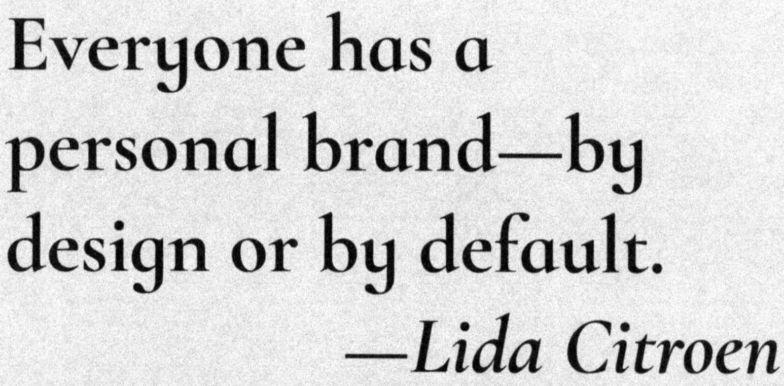

Everyone has a personal brand—by design or by default.

—*Lida Citroen*

29

If You Are Not a Brand, You Are a Commodity

A fundamental truth in sales is that people buy from people they like and trust to help them solve their problems. This is exactly what your personal brand should project.

Building the right personal brand reduces prospecting friction and elevates you above your competitors. It makes meeting with you and buying from you feel less risky than dealing with the competition.

An optimized personal brand creates inbound lead gravity—pulling prospects into your orbit. You don't chase attention; you attract it. And when the right people are paying attention, pipeline building gets much easier.

Think about it. When you send a connection request to a prospect, what's the first thing they do? They check your profile. When you show up in their feed, what shapes their perception of you? The quality of your content, the consistency of your activity, and the value you add.

A strong personal brand won't replace outbound prospecting—but it makes prospecting work better. It softens the ground before your cold call. It warms up the conversation before your discovery meeting. It keeps you top of mind when the buying window opens. And it supplements outbound activity with hot inbound leads.

A Level Playing Field

Not too long ago, if you wanted to build a personal brand, you had to *be somebody*. A big title. A big degree. A big-name company. You needed a good PR firm to do the heavy lifting. Publishing your thoughts was for the privileged few with money, agents, and access to media.

All that has changed. On LinkedIn, you can build tremendous visibility and authority without any of that. To become someone worth listening to, just show up consistently and share your ideas—as a teacher, advisor, problem solver, and resource.

LinkedIn gives every sales professional—regardless of seniority, geography, or company logo—the tools to build a brand. You don't need a marketing budget or a content team. All you need is a point of view combined with a little creativity, consistency, and courage.

Authority, earned through personal branding, is one of the most powerful edges you can create for yourself on LinkedIn.

Personal Branding Fuels Inbound Lead Gen

Jason sells into the cybersecurity space, which is a hyper-competitive market where it's crazy difficult to differentiate. To prospects, the companies and solutions in his industry all look the same. He was frustrated because it felt like he was being commoditized. Almost all prospecting conversations devolved into one question: "How much does it cost?"

After attending one of our LinkedIn Edge Boot Camps, he realized that in order to differentiate, he needed to become a red umbrella in a sea of gray suits. So he committed to building his personal brand on LinkedIn—one post, one comment, one helpful insight at a time.

He optimized his profile and then started sharing lessons from his conversations with CISOs (chief information security officers). He broke down complex frameworks into plain English and chimed in on industry posts.

Jason emphasized the importance of working with a trusted vendor, since companies are ultimately buying cybersecurity peace of mind. He discussed future trends, current threats, and the role of AI in network security.

His efforts gained attention. Within six months, his posts were being shared by industry thought leaders, he was being invited onto podcasts, and people were sending him connection requests with comments like "I really enjoy your take on the compliance side of cloud security."

Then leads began coming in. Prospects were contacting him to schedule sales calls. Rather than being commoditized as just another cybersecurity salesperson, Jason was being pulled into deeper conversations as a consultant, allowing him to shape buying decisions.

It wasn't magic. Jason had earned authority by showing up where his prospects were paying attention, making them smarter in the process.

This kind of professional presence doesn't happen by accident. It's built intentionally and systematically on LinkedIn. As Philip Kotler, the father of marketing, once said, "If you are not a brand, you are a commodity."

30

Personal Brand Audit

In our digital world, who you are online is who you are—at least to prospects. Your personal brand isn't what you say about yourself; in the words of Chris Ducker, "it's what people say about you when you are not in the room."

It's your reputation, your digital first impression, your influence footprint. And in B2B sales, your personal brand can be a force multiplier. It opens doors you didn't even know existed.

What must be understood, though, is that your personal brand is already forming, whether or not you are actively shaping it. Every comment, every post, every interaction builds a perception in the minds of your network connections, prospects, and customers. And, by the way, being absent from LinkedIn, or doing nothing, also shapes perception.

Start Your Personal Branding Journey with an Audit

The most effective way to begin your personal branding journey is through a personal brand audit. Start with four questions:

1. Is my personal brand working for me or against me?
2. Does my presence on LinkedIn support my reputation and credibility?
3. Does my current activity on LinkedIn help people become familiar with my name, face, and personal brand in a positive way?
4. Do I balance strengthening my personal brand with creating awareness for my product, service, or software and my company's brand?

If the answer to any of these questions is "no" or "I'm not sure," stop and make an adjustment in your strategy. Use the audit form in Exercise 30.1 as a guide.

EXERCISE 30.1 PERSONAL BRAND AUDIT CHECKLIST

Score each item from 1 (needs work) to 5 (strong), and add notes or action items where needed.

Audit Area	Score (1–5)	Notes/Action Steps
Google Results: Are the top results relevant and professional? Any outdated or off-brand content?		

(*Continued*)

(Continued)

SOCIAL MEDIA PROFILES AND CONTENT		
Social Media Visibility: Are your personal accounts aligned with your professional image? Anything you should hide or clean up?		
Content Tone and Topics: Does your posted or shared content reflect what you want to be known for?		
Consistency Across Platforms: Is your brand message consistent across LinkedIn, your website, and other platforms?		
LINKEDIN PROFILE		
Profile Image: Professional, current, and makes a great visual first impression?		

LINKEDIN PROFILE		
LinkedIn Profile Cover Image: Is it professional and current? Does it make a good visual first impression?		
Headline: Attention grabbing, keyword rich, and relevant?		
About Section: Focused on your value to others—not just your résumé?		
Featured Content: Are you showcasing posts, articles, or insights that reflect your expertise?		
Experience and Skills: Are your job history and skills current and relevant to your brand goals?		
Network Quality: Are you connected to the right people in your industry and market?		

(Continued)

(*Continued*)

COMPETITOR ANALYSIS AND PEER FEEDBACK		
Peer and Competitor Comparison: How do you stack up against competitors and peers in your industry?		
External Feedback: Ask others how you come across online. What did they say?		

As you complete your audit, make a list of the changes, actions, and updates you need to make in order to strengthen your personal brand.

Virtual First Impressions

Everyone makes quick judgments about people the first time they meet. To deal with an overwhelming amount of incoming data, your brain evolved to quickly look at patterns and compile that information into snapshots. These snapshots form your first impressions, regardless of how valid they may be.

Before meetings, stakeholders will look you up on LinkedIn in an effort to get the gist of who you are and what you are all about. They'll Google you, look at your headshot, read your headline, check out your "About" section bio, and review your posts.

Their judgments will impact your ability to influence them to commit time, resources, and money to you. It's difficult to change first impressions people make online because you often don't get a second chance. To avoid this fate, create an "online you" that reflects the professional story you want to tell.

Google Yourself

Start simple. Open a private browser tab. Type your name—and maybe your company name—into Google. Look at the first two pages of results. This is what your prospects see when they check you out.

- Are you showing up?
- Are the results professional and relevant?
- Are they consistent with how you want to be perceived?
- Are there outdated or off-brand links?
- Are your images appropriate for a business audience?
- How and where does your LinkedIn profile show up?

Evaluate Your LinkedIn Presence

LinkedIn is your primary sales storefront. It's the first place prospects go to size you up, so audit your profile with fresh eyes.

- Is your headline more than just your job title?
- Does your summary tell your story or read like a résumé?
- Are your featured sections highlighting your best work?
- Is your profile image current and professional?
- Are your skills and endorsements aligned with your role?

Now check your connections. Are they ICP decision-makers? Influencers? Referral partners? Or is your network full of random recruiters and forgotten classmates?

Review All Social Media Profiles

On each social media platform, you have a profile. It is your home base and personal branded page on that platform and in web search. Review each profile and gauge your visual first impression to ensure that your profiles cast you in the best light.

- Your headshots are current and professional
- Profile cover images support your personal and company brand
- Profile bios and headlines are complete, truthful, and tell your story well
- Profile keywords make it easy for people to find you in search
- You project a consistent personal brand across all major social networks

Review Public Content

Review the content that you have posted across all of your public social media accounts including LinkedIn. Ask yourself:

- Does this content reflect my expertise?
- Does my tone match the professional image I'm building?
- Am I contributing insights—or just adding noise?
- Could any of my posts alienate potential buyers or cause them to judge me as incompetent, toxic, or worse?

Go back years. Delete or edit anything that doesn't align with the brand you want to project. If you don't have time to remove it or don't want to, then set those accounts to private and restrict who can see them.

You don't have to scrub your personality—but you do have to protect your professional reputation.

People Do Not Make the Distinction Between Personal and Business Posts

Not long ago, a well-known author asked Jeb for an endorsement— a blurb for the back of his new book and website. He sent over an early copy, and based on the quality of the writing, Jeb was inclined to say yes. But before finalizing his decision, Jeb did a quick scan of the author's online presence.

The author's social feeds were a firestorm—emotionally charged, laced with profanity, and overflowing with political rants. Many of the posts directly contradicted the values Jeb holds personally and the standards his team lives by at Sales Gravy. It wasn't just unprofessional—it was polarizing.

Jeb stepped back and considered the potential impact. What if a client saw his name on the book and looked up the author? What would his team think? How would it reflect on his brand?

In the end, Jeb made the call to politely decline the endorsement. The author didn't take it well. He argued it was his "First Amendment right" to post whatever he wanted and that it had nothing to do with business. But for Jeb, it had everything to do with business, and endorsing the book could be seen as endorsing all of the author's opinions.

Manage Everything You Allow Others to See

When it comes to your personal brand, people viewing your social media presence do not make the distinction between personal and business. If you wish to sell books, software, products, or services, it is just dead stupid to post anything that might turn off potential buyers.

For this reason, you must carefully manage everything you allow other people to see on social media. You must refrain from posting anything that could be considered controversial.

As sales professionals, we must consider the potential impact of things we post—to our credibility, reputation, and income. There's no such thing as "just personal" when it comes to your online footprint.

Everything you post becomes part of your brand—whether you like it or not. In sales, all publicity is *not* good publicity.

In other words, if you like money, don't post dumb stuff on social media.

Define the Brand You Want to Build

Before you start posting or overhauling your profile, take a step back. Get clear on what you want to be known for:

- What's the intersection of your expertise, your passions, and your market's problems?
- What kind of opportunities do you want your brand to attract?
- Who do you want to influence?

This clarity will guide you as you elevate your LinkedIn profile and will shape your posts, comments, and shares. It is key to setting effective goals for building your personal brand and authority.

EXERCISE 30.2 DEFINE YOUR DESIRED PERSONAL BRAND

Personal Brand Question	Your Answer
What three to five words do I want people to associate with me professionally?	
What am I an expert in?	
What do I want to be known for?	
What types of people or companies do I want to attract?	
What kind of content or topics do I want to own?	
What are the keywords people will use in search to find me?	

Get Another Set of Eyeballs

It's always a good idea to get another perspective. Ask three trusted colleagues, friends, clients, or even your significant other to give you their perspective on your personal brand:

- What do you think I'm known for?
- What's your impression of my LinkedIn presence?
- How does my personal brand come across on other social media platforms?
- If you were introducing me to someone, how would you describe what I do?

Listen closely. The truth might surprise you—and it'll absolutely sharpen your strategy.

Analyze Competitors

Pick three professionals in your industry whose personal brands you admire. Study their presence:

- What kind of content are they posting?
- How do they engage with others?
- What's their tone, positioning, frequency?
- What makes them credible?

Don't copy them, but learn from them. Look for gaps in your own presence where you could raise the bar.

Set Your Personal Brand Goals

A strong personal brand doesn't happen by accident. You build it brick by brick, over time. So set clear, measurable goals:

- How often will you post?
- What topics will you become known for?
- What content formats will you focus on?

Track your progress monthly. Tweak your approach. Stay consistent. The goal isn't to be famous. It's to be *familiar* and *trusted* by the people who matter most.

EXERCISE 30.3 PERSONAL BRAND GOALS

Stop and set your personal branding activity goals. Do the work now, and your future self will thank you.

Area	Goal	Action Steps
Posting Frequency		
LinkedIn Profile Visits		
Network Growth		
Comments		
Shares		
Mentions		
Content Strategy		
Search Visibility		
Inbound Leads		

31

The LinkedIn Profile Makeover

Your LinkedIn profile is different from your résumé. It needs to sell who you are, what you know, and how you help—not where you've been. It must speak directly to the problems your prospects are trying to solve right now. It must trigger curiosity, invite conversation, demonstrate authority, and position you as a trusted expert.

Your LinkedIn profile is your digital storefront. And like any good storefront, it needs to be designed with your customer in mind. When your profile makes your value obvious, when it gives people a reason to pause, read, and learn, you open the door to more conversations, credibility, and opportunities.

You don't need to be a LinkedIn guru or hire a copywriter to make your profile pop. You just need to follow a simple, proven process that helps you clarify your message and tell the right story to the right people.

Over the course of the next few chapters we'll walk you through the process of transforming your LinkedIn profile from a digital business card into a dynamic asset that becomes the core foundation of your personal brand, and becomes an inbound lead machine.

Grabbing Attention Above the Fold

Before anyone scrolls through your LinkedIn profile, they've already made a snap judgment. If it doesn't grab attention in those first crucial seconds, you lose them.

That's the power—and the danger—of what's known as the "above the fold" section of your LinkedIn profile. It's the first thing a visitor sees when they land on your page. Your name, headline, photo, background image, and contact details are all right there, front and center.

Every element of the above the fold section of your LinkedIn profile needs to work together to tell people exactly who you are, what you do, and why they should care.

Step 1: Save Your Profile Before Editing

Since LinkedIn lacks an "undo" option, before you make any modifications, download your profile as a PDF:

1. Go to your LinkedIn profile.
2. Click on "More" (under your profile image) and choose "Save to PDF."
3. Keep it in an easily accessible place for future reference.

This acts as a safeguard in case you want to reinstate earlier content and is a benchmark reference as you make changes.

Step 2: Cover Image Banner

It all starts with your *cover image*. This is prime digital real estate—your personal billboard. Your banner should tell a story the moment someone lands on your profile. Do not leave it blank or use generic stock images.

Think of it as a visual handshake. It should reflect your brand, your company, and your value. Incorporate your organization's colors, messaging, and personality.

Highlight upcoming events, webinars, or key announcements. Switch it out based on what you're promoting or where you're showing up.

LinkedIn Premium allows users to upload up to five rotating banners—like a mini slideshow. Use that feature to spotlight your expertise, reinforce brand messaging, and keep your profile dynamic and engaging.

Upload Your Cover Image to LinkedIn

1. Go to your profile.
2. If you're doing this for the first time, click on the camera icon in the top-right of the cover image area. To replace an existing banner, click on the pencil icon in the top-right corner of the cover image area.
3. Click "Upload Photo" or "Create a Slideshow" (for premium members).
4. Select the banner file you saved on your computer.
5. Crop the photo, use photo filters, adjust, change the position and size, or rotate your cover image as needed, then click "Apply."
6. View your profile and continue to adjust until you have it dialed in.

Design Your Banner in Canva

In our opinion, Canva is hands down the best tool for building your cover image banner. Every sales pro should have an account and know how to use it.

1. Set up a free account on Canva.com.

2. To use a pre-sized template, visit https://www.canva.com/create/linkedin-banners/.

3. Build your cover image banner.

If you create your cover image on a different platform, follow these image specifications:

- Use a JPG or PNG file type.
- Keep the file size under 8MB.
- Dimensions should be 1584 × 396 pixels.

Step 3: Headshot

Your headshot is the first visual cue people get about you—and it matters more than most salespeople think. According to PhotoFeeler.com, "Profile photos are so essential to modern communication that a good one becomes a basic necessity. And that couldn't be truer than for those of us whose professional lives are tied to social media profiles."

This isn't the place for a selfie, an AI avatar, a cropped wedding photo, or your favorite tailgate memory. No cats, no kids, no beer bottles, and definitely no mirror pics from your gym. A professional headshot—one that looks like the person who will show up to the meeting—is nonnegotiable.

It should be taken in good lighting, at a flattering angle, and on a clean, neutral background. Drop the cheesy poses: no crossed arms, chin grabs, or staring wistfully into the horizon. You're not auditioning for a cologne ad. These poses make you come off like a self-centered schmuck.

Instead, look directly into the camera. Be open. Be approachable. And smile—genuinely. PhotoFeeler analyzed over 60,000 ratings and found that a real, confident smile significantly boosts perceived competence, likability, and influence.

Few things create a positive impression faster than a warm, sincere smile.

If you've updated your look—shaved a beard, changed your hairstyle, switched up your glasses—update your photo. The goal is for your prospects to instantly recognize you when your meeting starts. That recognition, even subconsciously, builds comfort. And comfort builds connection.

Upload Your Headshot to LinkedIn

1. Go to your profile.
2. Click your existing photo (or the photo placeholder if you don't have one yet).
3. Click "add photo."
4. Upload your new photo.
5. Crop, edit, and adjust as needed: using the cropping tool to center your face and the built-in zoom, rotate, and filters, as needed.
6. Set your photo to public for visibility and branding (unless there is a security reason that you need to make your photo private).
7. Once you're happy with the image and settings, click "Save photo."

For best results, use the same headshot across all your social platforms: LinkedIn, X (formerly Twitter), Instagram, Facebook, Slack, Zoom—you name it. Your image is like your logo. Repetition builds familiarity. Familiarity builds trust. And trust opens doors.

Step 4: Headline

A few months back, right before the start of a LinkedIn Edge workshop for commercial bankers, a veteran banker named Eric pulled aside Jack—our instructor—with a skeptical tone.

"Are you the one running this class?" he asked. Jack nodded. "My president forced me to be here," Eric grumbled. The message was clear: I'm not buying what you're selling.

Later, when the group reviewed profile headlines, Jack noticed that Eric's simply read: "Vice President, Commercial Lender."

"How do you feel about it?" Jack asked.

"I love it," Eric said with a hint of arrogance.

Jack didn't flinch. "There are around 100,000 people in the US with that same title. If you want to blend in, that's fine. But is that really what you want?"

Eric paused. "No. I want to stand out. I want to be seen as the banker who gets it done for my clients."

"Perfect," Jack said. "Let's try something different. How about: 'The Banker in Charge of Getting Things Done in Hartford'?"

Eric laughed. "That sounds ridiculous. But fine—I'll give it 30 days."

Thirty days later, Eric emailed Jack in disbelief. "You won't believe this. I had three people reach out to talk about banking. One CFO even said he'd been looking his whole career for a banker who gets things done."

Your LinkedIn headline is prime real estate. At just 220 characters, it's one of the most valuable pieces of digital property you own. And yet most sales professionals squander it by listing nothing more than their job title and company name.

"Sales Manager at XYZ Corp" won't cut it. That headline puts you in the pile with every other sales manager out there. It doesn't speak to who you help, how you help them, or why anyone should care.

Your headline is your positioning statement. Think of it as your elevator pitch in a sentence—a clear, concise signal that grabs attention and says, "This is who I help, and here's how I do it."

When your headline is written right, it sparks curiosity, establishes credibility, and starts conversations. And when people are scrolling LinkedIn, your headline—along with your photo and name—is what determines whether they click or keep scrolling.

The Headline Formula: Who You Help + Outcomes You Deliver + How You Help

Use this simple framework to guide your headline: I help [Target Audience] [Achieve Outcomes] by [What You Do].

Here are some examples:

- Helping CFOs in SaaS Startups Reduce Burn and Scale Confidently with Fractional Finance Leadership.

- I Help Sales Teams Shorten the Sales Cycle and Close More Deals Through Practical Training and Coaching.

- Equipping Construction Leaders with the Tools to Hire Smarter and Build Faster.

- Helping B2B Sales Teams Master Prospecting and Close More Deals Through Practical, No-Fluff Sales Training.

- Empowering IT Leaders to Reduce Downtime and Boost Productivity Through AI-Powered Network Solutions.

- Helping CMOs Win Budget Battles with Metrics-Driven Campaigns That Deliver Real Results.

- Helping Startup Founders Sleep at Night by Building Financial Models, Forecasts, and Systems that Scale.

Avoid buzzwords. Focus on clarity, specificity, and outcomes.

How to Update Your LinkedIn Headline

Done right, your headline becomes a conversation starter, a credibility builder, and a magnet for the right kind of attention. Take these steps to get started:

1. Go to your profile.
2. Click the pencil icon near your name and headline.
3. In the Headline field, delete your current text and add your new positioning statement. (Keep it under 220 characters—including spaces.)
4. Click "Save."

Revisit your headline every 6–12 months to make sure it still reflects who you help, how you help, and the value you deliver today—not who you were two jobs ago.

Step 5: Name Pronunciation and Elevator Pitch

LinkedIn's Name Pronunciation feature is about more than phonetics. It's an underrated opportunity to stand out.

In 10 seconds, you can instantly make your profile warmer, more human, and more memorable. When used strategically, this feature becomes a mini elevator pitch—spoken in your own voice—that reinforces who you help and the value you bring. Use it to:

- Clearly pronounce your name so there's no guesswork.
- Offer a short, human-centered positioning statement.

Here's an example: "Hi, I'm Brynne Tillman. I help B2B sales teams use LinkedIn to start better conversations without sounding salesy."

How to Record Your Name Pronunciation

You can only add this feature using the LinkedIn mobile app.

1. Open the LinkedIn app on your phone.
2. Tap your profile photo in the top left, then tap "View Profile."
3. Tap the pencil icon next to your profile photo.
4. Scroll down to "Name Pronunciation" and tap the microphone to record.
5. Speak clearly and slowly—you only get 10 seconds.
6. Save the recording and preview it to make sure it sounds right.

Practice your pitch a few times before recording. Be natural. Smile. Speak like you would in a first meeting. That's what makes it stick.

This little audio clip adds warmth and personality to your digital presence and creates an audio brand and voiceprint that prospects remember.

Step 6: Make It Easy to Contact You

When a prospect is ready to take the next step, make it easy for them to reach you. Nothing stalls inbound lead momentum faster than a missing phone number or email.

- Start with your email. Use a professional address that builds trust. That means yourname@company.com, not salesguy 1978@gmail.com.

- Add links to your website, calendar, lead magnet, blog, or podcast. This is where you point people who are interested in learning more or booking time with you. Treat it like your call-to-action space.

- Finally, add your phone number. Some sales professionals hesitate to include it. Don't. You are in sales. Your phone ringing is the goal.

- If you're concerned about privacy, use a VoIP number like Google Voice or OpenPhone. That way, you stay accessible without handing out your personal number.

- Add your birthday month and day. Each year, when people drop in to say happy birthday, use that moment to reconnect and deepen the relationship. It's one of the easiest and most organic ways to gain visibility.

How to Update Your LinkedIn Contact Information

The bottom line is that your contact info needs to be complete, current, and visible to your connections. Buyers shouldn't have to dig. When they're ready, you need to be ready.

1. Go to your profile.
2. At the top-right corner, next to your photo and headline, click the pencil icon to open the profile editor.
3. In the profile editor, scroll until you see the contact info section. Click the pencil icon next to it.
4. Add your professional email (yourname@company.com) and set it as your primary. You can associate multiple emails with your LinkedIn account, but your primary email is what connections see.

5. Enter your business mobile, office, or VoIP number. Be sure to select the correct country code.

6. You can add multiple links under "Website." Use descriptive labels like "Company Website," "Schedule a Call," or "Download My Guide."

7. Add your birthday. LinkedIn will notify your connections on your special day and create an opportunity for reengagement.

8. Once you've updated your information, click "Save."

9. You can also adjust who can see each piece of contact information. Set visibility to "Your connections" for professional access, or "Only you" if you're storing info for your own records.

Remember, if people can't easily contact you they may just move on.

32

The Middle Hooks

Once you've grabbed your profile visitor's attention with the above-the-fold elements, the real work begins. Now you've got to hook them. To make them stop scrolling and think, "This person gets it. This person understands me."

The middle section of your LinkedIn profile is where interest turns into intent. It's the meat of your profile—the substance behind the sizzle. It's where you back up your headline and prove that you're more than just a clever tagline.

This is your LinkedIn profile lead-generation engine. Here's where the real story gets told—who you help, how you help, why it matters, and what makes you different. The middle of your profile includes four core sections:

- **About:** This is your story. It's where you connect the dots between your audience's challenges and the outcomes you deliver. Done right, it positions you as a guide they can trust.

- **Featured:** Your proof zone. Showcase content, wins, or resources that build authority and back up your brand promise. This is also a place where you can generate inbound leads.
- **Services:** A short list of what you actually do. This makes it easy for people to quickly understand how they can work with you.
- **Activity:** This section showcases your LinkedIn posts, comments, videos, images, articles, and documents.

The good news for you is that most LinkedIn profile middles are dull, self-centered, and completely forgettable, which means that when you do it right, you own the room.

Step 7: Tell Your Story in the About Section

Most LinkedIn About sections are a bland wall of text packed with career highlights, job titles, and word-salad jargon no buyer cares about. It's a résumé in disguise. It's boring. And that's exactly why no one reads it.

Your prospects aren't scrolling LinkedIn looking for someone with "20 years of experience" or a string of awards. They're looking for someone who can solve a problem. Period.

This isn't the place to prove you're qualified. It's the place to prove you understand the challenges, pain, and problems faced by your target ICP prospects and stakeholders.

The About section is your hook. It's your chance to grab your buyer by their heart and say, "I hear you. I get it. I've seen this before. And I can help."

When you speak their language—when you show them that you get their pain and that you've got the answers—you become someone worth talking to. If your About section isn't doing this, it's costing you leads.

Leverage the PIPA Framework to Craft a Scroll-Stopping About Section

The best About sections meet your prospect where they are—inside their problems—and walk them straight to a solution that you are uniquely positioned to provide.

The *PIPA framework* gives you a simple structure for crafting powerful, relevant messaging that hooks attention, builds authority, and compels action.

P = Pain

Start by naming the core problem your ideal customer is facing. Be specific. This is how you signal, "I get you." For example:

> *Most founders hit a wall when it's time to scale. The books are a mess. Cash flow's unpredictable. Financial decisions are based on gut feel—not data. And the stress? It's constant.*

Enter the conversation that is already happening in your prospect's mind. The more clearly you articulate their pain, the more they'll believe you can solve it. The key is stepping into their shoes and leveraging empathy to view the situation through their lens.

I = Insight

Next, share a sharp, experience-backed insight that reframes the problem—or shows your prospect a better path. This is where you earn credibility by showing you understand how to solve their problem at a deeper level. For example:

> *You don't need more spreadsheets—you need clarity. Real visibility into what's working, what's broken, and where your business is bleeding cash. The right financial strategy makes decisions easier, faster, and way more profitable.*

Insight proves you're not just another vendor. You're someone who knows how to solve problems.

P = Position

Now position yourself as uniquely qualified to help them solve the problem you just described. Keep it crisp, human, and focused on outcomes. For example:

> *I help founders of high-growth startups take control of their finances so that they can scale faster, while assuring investors that they are in control, with fractional CFO support that's hands-on, founder-friendly, and built for speed.*

This isn't a product pitch. It's a positioning statement. It answers the question *Why should I trust you to solve this for me?*

A = Action

Finish strong with a simple, clear call to action. Don't beg. Don't pitch. Just open the door.

> *If you're navigating growth and the numbers are starting to feel like quicksand, let's talk. Whether or not we work together, I'll share some best practices that will help you make sense of the numbers and gain peace of mind.*
> ✉ [Email] | ☎ [Phone Number] | 📅 [Calendar Link]

How to edit your LinkedIn About section

1. Go to your profile.
2. Scroll to the "About" section. If you don't have one yet, LinkedIn will prompt you to "Add About." If it's already there, you'll see a pencil icon in the upper-right corner of the section. This opens the editor, where you can write or update your About section.

3. Write or paste your copy.

4. Check the formatting. Use short paragraphs, white space, and occasional line breaks for readability. Bullet points or bold text won't format in this section, so structure matters.

5. Click "Save." Once you're happy with it, click the blue Save button. Your About section is now live.

6. Review on mobile. View your profile on your phone to make sure the formatting looks clean. Most people will check you out on mobile first.

About Section Examples and AI Prompts

Here you'll find examples of effective About statements and an AI prompt framework to help you get started elevating yours.

Example 1: Business Development Rep/Fleet Solutions Consultant

Pain: Managing a fleet is expensive, time-consuming, and full of hidden risks. Maintenance delays. Compliance headaches. Unexpected breakdowns. It all slows you down and drains your bottom line.

Insight: Most companies think they're saving money by owning trucks. But when you add up the real costs—capital, downtime, lost productivity, new technology, emissions compliance—leasing starts to look like the smarter move.

Position: I help fleet managers, logistics teams, and operations leaders move from chaos to control with full-service truck leasing and maintenance solutions.

Action: If you're exploring ways to improve uptime, reduce costs, or scale faster, let's talk. I'll help you break it down so you can make a smarter decision.

✉ [Email] | ☎ [Phone Number] | 📅 [Calendar Link]

Example 2: Construction Equipment, Territory Sales Representative

Pain: Downtime eats profits. And when equipment fails, delays follow. Projects fall behind, crews get frustrated, and revenue slips through your fingers.

Insight: The right machine isn't just a tool—it's a partner in productivity. And a good partner should keep you running, competitive, and profitable.

Position: I work with contractors and construction leaders to equip their teams with machines that deliver performance, reliability, and ROI—backed by the service and support to keep jobs on track.

Action: If you're planning a purchase, lease or reviewing your fleet strategy, I'd be happy to walk you through options that fit your work and your margins.

✉ [Email] | ☎ [Phone Number] | 📅 [Calendar Link]

Example 3: IT Consultant for Healthcare Systems

Pain: Many healthcare IT systems are bloated, slow, and stitched together with legacy software. Providers spend more time fighting the tools than serving patients.

Insight: Technology should enable better care—not block it. Smart integration, streamlined workflows, and modern platforms unlock speed and precision where it matters most.

Position: I work with healthcare organizations to modernize their IT infrastructure—cutting complexity, reducing risk, and freeing up teams to focus on care.

Action: If your systems are slowing you down, let's talk. A 20-minute strategy call could uncover weeks' worth of operational gains.

✉ [Email] | ☎ [Phone Number] | 📅 [Calendar Link]

Your About section isn't your pitch—it's *your prospect's reason* to engage with you. Use the PIPA framework. Speak their language. Keep it real and relevant. When you do this right, more prospects and hot leads will come to you.

Step 8: Elevate the Featured Section

Your Featured section is your scroll-stopper—a powerful highlight reel of your professional story. It's your own personal sales page and lead-generation magnet baked right into your LinkedIn profile. Sadly, it is the one section most frequently ignored or suboptimized by sales professionals.

Take Andrew, for example—a sales rep for a rising tech company. He used his Featured section to showcase a killer client success story. The post walked readers through how he helped his customer dramatically boost brand engagement. It wasn't braggy—it was relevant. It told a story. And it was backed by measurable business outcomes.

Then he pinned it in his Featured section. A few weeks later, a prospect who'd been quietly vetting vendors reached out. Why? Because his story answered the question every buyer is silently asking: *Can this person actually help me?*

This is the power of the Featured section. It's visual social proof, credibility, and authority all wrapped up in a beautiful package that you control.

What you should feature:

- High-performing posts that drive engagement or conversation.
- How-to articles that educate with insights and your industry expertise.
- Customer success stories or testimonials that highlight real results and relationships.
- Videos and micro-demos.
- Lead magnets, including downloadable resources, guides, or checklists.
- Webinar or podcast links of appearances or content that builds your credibility.
- Scheduling link to make it easy for someone to take the next step.

This Is Your Highlight Reel

If your headline gets them curious, and your About section draws them in, the Featured section is your highlight reel, which makes them think, "This is someone I need to talk to."

It's important to refresh this section regularly so that there is always something new.

How to add or edit your Featured section

1. Go to Your Profile.

2. Scroll to the Featured section. If it's not there, click "Add profile section," then "Recommended," and choose "Add featured."

3. Click the + icon to add a:
   - LinkedIn post
   - Article
   - External link
   - Media (PDF, presentation, etc.)

4. Rearrange items by dragging and dropping to feature your strongest content first.

5. Refresh regularly to reflect your most relevant, recent work.

Step 9: Leverage the Services Section

The Services section on your LinkedIn profile is an underutilized business development tool available to sales professionals, consultants, and service providers. This section allows you to use rich media to articulate value clarity and explain exactly how you help your clients.

Why leveraging the Services section matters

- **Boosts your discoverability:** LinkedIn's algorithm favors profiles that contain a Services section. When your section includes relevant keywords and content, you're more likely to surface in searches.

- **Qualifies you in:** Prospects aren't just reading profiles—they're qualifying vendors. Clear service descriptions and rich media make it easier to trust that you and your company know what you're doing.

- **Provides instant clarity:** When a buyer hits your profile, they're asking, "Can this person help me?" Your Services section helps them answer that question in the affirmative faster.

- **Reinforces your positioning:** When paired with your headline, About section, and Featured content, the Services section rounds out your message: *I help people like you solve problems like this, and here is how I actually do it.*

How to set up or update your Services section

1. Go to Your LinkedIn profile.
2. Click the "Add Profile Section" button underneath your headline.
3. Select "Add Services."
4. Choose your industry and services from LinkedIn's predefined list.
5. Write a short, tight description (500-character max) that focuses on: Who you help, how you help, the outcomes you create. Treat this as an extension of your About statement.
6. Add rich media (up to eight assets)—videos, client testimonials, PDF downloads, event recordings, or media mentions.
7. Click "Publish."

Review your Services section often and update to keep it fresh and relevant.

Step 10: Check Your Activity Section—Are You Showing Up or Sitting Out?

Your Activity section is the visible proof that you're present, engaged, and adding value on the LinkedIn platform. It is your thought leadership and personal branding breadcrumb trail.

Buyers are checking it. Before they respond to your connection request, before they reply to your message, before they book that meeting—they scroll straight to this section to get a glimpse of what you are all about.

And the Activity section doesn't lie. It answers one of the most important questions on your buyer's mind: Is this person legit?

How to audit and improve your Activity section

1. Go to your profile.

2. Scroll to your Activity section.

3. Click "See all activity" to review everything you've posted, liked, and commented on.

4. Ask yourself:
   - Would I trust or follow this person?
   - Does this activity align with my personal brand?
   - Am I showing up as a helpful expert?

5. If you don't like what you see, fix it:
   - Leave thoughtful comments on two or three industry-relevant posts per day.
   - Post original content once or twice a week (even short-form works).
   - Reshare content with context—add your take; don't just click "Share."

If you're not showing up, if your last post was from six months ago, or your only engagement is a handful of likes on company announcements, your prospects notice.

When a decision-maker is vetting you, your activity feed becomes a window into your thinking—and a mirror of your credibility. It's where your personal brand is in motion. It's the proof that you think like they think, speak their language, and understand their world.

33

Credentials and Credibility

As stakeholders decide if they should meet with you, give you information, move to the next step, evaluate your proposal and business case, compare you to your competitors, and ultimately make the decision to do business with you, they are—consciously and subconsciously—assessing the risk that doing so might harm them.

People Don't Like Change

The number one reason why buyers choose not to move forward with you is not price, product specs, delivery windows, competitors, or any of the things salespeople too often blame. It's the fear of negative future consequences.

Your prospects live with an underlying fear that change will make things worse. In his book *Thinking, Fast and Slow*, Daniel Kahneman, the father of heuristic psychology, writes:

Organisms that placed more urgency on avoiding threats than they did maximizing opportunities were more likely to pass on their genes. So, over time, the prospect of losses has become a more powerful motivator on your behavior than the promise of gains[1].

This safety bias causes your buyer's brain to be more aware of what could go wrong than what can go right. They are hyper-tuned-into anything about you that is negative. They gravitate toward safe choices.

Emotional Baggage

Salespeople, as a rule, are not perceived as safe. You pose a threat. Your buyers are worried. "What if we make a change and things go wrong?" They worry that you won't live up to your promises, that you'll disrupt their business, that you'll manipulate them.

And why shouldn't they? The salespeople who came before you failed them when it mattered most.

Buyers remember negative past experiences more vividly than positive ones, and bring this emotional baggage into their interactions with you, thus magnifying every flaw, concern, and incongruence they find about you.

This is why it is a guarantee that every stakeholder will review your LinkedIn profile every time. And when they do, they will not be looking for what is right about you—they will be looking for what is wrong.

---

[1] Daniel Kahneman, *Thinking, Fast and Slow* (Farrar, Straus and Giroux, 2013).

De-risk Yourself

The bottom third of your LinkedIn profile is where you de-risk yourself in the minds of prospects and referral partners.

Everything you've done to this point—your headline, your About section, your Featured content—has been about earning attention. But sales is a trust game. Always has been.

The bottom third of your profile is where you shift the focus from interesting and credible to safe, capable, and trustworthy—proof that you've done this before, people trust you, and others have put their reputations on the line to endorse you.

You're not just telling your story here. You're removing doubt and breaking through cynicism, skepticism, and distrust with compelling evidence that you are the real deal.

Credibility Sections

There are five key sections in this part of your profile that work together to tip the scales in your favor:

- **Experience:** This is more than a list of job titles. It's a credibility narrative. Each role should reinforce your relevance, your expertise, and your impact. Prospects want to see that you've walked the walk—and that others have trusted you in roles that matter.

- **Education:** It's not just about degrees. It's about shaping context. Education signals discipline, commitment, and the lens through which you see the world.

- **Licenses and certifications:** These badges tell the buyer, "I've been tested. I've earned this." If your industry has standards, show others that you've met or exceeded them.

- **Skills:** When aligned with your messaging and endorsed by others, skills create micro-validations that reinforce your credibility and improve your ranking in search results.
- **Recommendations:** These are gold. In a world full of puffed-up claims, recommendations are social proof. They're third-party credibility from people who've worked with you, bought from you, or trusted you enough to put it in writing.

When optimized, these five sections turn you from a question mark into a safe bet. They become your digital trust signals. And in a world where attention is short and skepticism is high, trust is the ultimate competitive advantage.

Step 11: Build Out Your Experience

Your Experience section is where you de-risk yourself by demonstrating that you've helped others like your prospect, and that you know how to deliver results.

This is the section where you show your work. Forget copy-pasting your job description. Nobody cares. Your prospects don't want a laundry list of tasks—they want proof. Proof that you've solved problems like theirs, understand their industry, and working with you is a safe bet.

In one of our LinkedIn Edge workshops, Regina, a SaaS account executive, rewrote her Experience section to tell her story rather than list duties. She told the story of how she helped clients implement solutions that drove efficiency, cut churn, and generated real ROI.

Two weeks later, a prospect mentioned it during a call, "I saw your profile before we met. I liked what you did with that client in logistics. We've got a similar challenge."

That's the difference. When your profile is written from the buyer's point of view, you're no longer just another rep. You're a professional who *gets them.*

Example Experience Section (the Right Way)

Account Executive | SaaS Sales Specialist | Helping Growth-Stage Companies Scale with Confidence

Company:
XSaaSAI Solutions
January 2021–Present

Description:
I help business leaders streamline operational workflows, reduce headcount, and grow revenue through tailored technology solutions. My approach is consultative—because no two businesses are the same.

From the first conversation, I work to understand what's holding your team back. Then I share insights and strategies based on what's worked for similar clients—always focused on solving *your* specific challenges.

Here are a few recent wins:

- Helped a logistics firm increase inbound lead conversion by 40 percent through optimized sales enablement workflows

- Guided 20-plus enterprise clients through implementation, reducing churn by 25 percent and accelerating time-to-value

- Delivered over $1M in net-new revenue to client portfolios through smart tech positioning and ROI-focused conversations

- Partnered with marketing to boost engagement by 30 percent, resulting in more qualified conversations and shorter sales cycles

The results speak for themselves. But more importantly, so do my clients.

> **AI PRO TIP**
>
> **Experience Prompt 1:** As a [job title] in [industry], I want my LinkedIn Experience section to reflect the way I listen, diagnose problems, and guide buyers toward solutions. Create a profile entry that focuses less on selling and more on helping.
>
> **Experience Prompt 2:** Write a LinkedIn Experience entry for my role as a [job title] at [company name]. Focus on how I help my customers. Include who I serve, the problems I solve, the outcomes I deliver, and specific results. Make it sound like it was written for my buyers—not for a hiring manager.
>
> **Experience Prompt 3:** Write my LinkedIn Experience section with a focus on storytelling and relevance to potential clients. Start by helping me articulate my "why" in the style of Simon Sinek—clarify:
>
> Why do I do what I do?
>
> What motivates me to serve this market?
>
> Why did I choose this company or role?
>
> Next, create a professional title and SEO-friendly tagline (format: **TITLE | Keywords**) for my profile. Once approved, write my full Experience section using this structure:
>
> Open with my "why"—what drives me in this work.
>
> Explain what my company does and why I chose to join it.
>
> *(Continued)*

(*Continued*)

Highlight how I help clients, including problems I solve.

Include client-focused outcomes or proof points.

Share what I love about working in this role.

Close with a call to connect or a link to my website.

Here's what you'll need from me to get started:

- My current job title and company
- Who I serve (target audience or ICP)
- What problems I solve
- A story or example of client success (optional)
- My company or personal website URL (optional)
- Whether I want the tone to be friendly, formal, or conversational

Add Rich Media, Links, and Content That Proves Your Value

LinkedIn gives you the opportunity to level up your Experience section with links, images, videos, documents, and presentations add to each role in your Experience section. This is a powerful way to go beyond telling and show people why you can be trusted by including:

- Customer success stories or case studies
- Slide decks from webinars or product demos
- Whitepapers or e-books you contributed to
- Links to press features or podcast appearances
- Video testimonials or explainer videos

Adding media brings your story to life. It gives your prospects something to explore—and builds confidence that you're the real deal.

How to Edit Your Experience Section on LinkedIn

1. Go to your profile.

2. Scroll to the "Experience" section.

3. Add or edit a role:
   - To add a new role: Click the "+" icon in the top-right corner of the Experience section.
   - To edit an existing role: Click the pencil icon next to the job you want to update.

4. Update your title, company, and timeframe. Use a positioning statement in your job title. For example, instead of just "Account Executive" write:

   Account Executive | SaaS Specialist | Driving Digital Transformation for Healthcare Providers

5. Tell your story in the description field. This is where you make it count. Use the Challenge, Solution, Outcome micro-story format:
   - Identify the challenges your customers faced.
   - Explain how you helped them.
   - Articulate the specific outcomes they derived from your solution.

6. Add skills to make your experience keyword rich, searchable, and easy to scan.

7. Scroll down to the "Media" section at the bottom of the job listing.

8. Click "Upload" to add a file (PDF, PPT, JPG, etc.), or "Link" to add a URL.

9. Add a title and description to explain what the viewer is seeing—and make it count. Use keywords and include your role in the project or outcome.

10. Save and review your work.

When you combine powerful messaging with rich content, your Experience section becomes a proof point that sets you apart.

Step 12: Optimize Your Education Entries

Your education section signals credibility, discipline, and your professional journey—it's far more than just a list of degrees. Instead of simply listing school names and dates, use this valuable real estate to differentiate yourself and add dimension to your profile.

Highlight the schools and programs that shaped you, but take it a step further by adding relevant context. Did you complete a senior project that relates to the work you do now? Did you lead an organization, publish research, or win a leadership award? These details help bring your academic experience to life.

Even better, enhance these entries with rich media. Upload a photo from a keynote you gave on campus. Link to a research article or capstone project. Add a video from a business competition or club presentation. This type of media turns your education from background noise into visual proof of who you are and what you've accomplished.

You can even include the work you do at your alma mater as an alumni. For example, Jeb gave the commencement speech at his university. Education doesn't need to sit silently at the bottom of your profile. Use it to entice connection and reinforce your credibility.

Step 13: Add Licenses and Certifications That Mean Something

The licenses and certifications section is where you tell the world: I've done the work, earned the credentials, and I'm qualified.

For sales professionals, this section is often underutilized or bloated with irrelevant fluff. You don't need 50 badges—just the ones that matter. Prioritize certifications that:

- Are relevant to your role, industry, or solution
- Signal a level of trust, skill, or authority
- Give prospects confidence in your credibility
- Align with keywords that improve your position in search results

Include industry-specific programs, technical credentials, relevant product certifications, and courses that deepen your value in the eyes of prospects. If you're certified in a selling methodology (like SPIN, MEDDIC, Challenger, Sales EQ, or Fanatical Prospecting), list it. If you've completed a course on Sales Gravy University, add it, especially if it aligns with your current role. Always include:

- The issuing organization
- A brief, compelling description of what the certification covers
- Any relevant links or supporting material
- When possible, add a link or upload your certificate

Here again you have the opportunity to add rich media that supports your credentials. Take advantage of it. That visual stamp of credibility goes a long way when someone is sizing you up at a glance. It tells decision-makers that you're a serious professional, invested in your craft, and continually sharpening your edge.

Step 14: Skills and Endorsements

The skills section is fuel for LinkedIn's search engine. These skills and keywords are also indexed on Google, Bing, and AI search engines like ChatGPT, Perplexity, and Gemini.

The right keywords in your skills section can make the difference between getting found or getting overlooked. LinkedIn lets you list up to 50 skills. Don't waste that real estate. Stack it with relevant, high-impact skills that align with what your buyers are searching for. If you want to show up when your prospect searches for "fractional CFO," "enterprise SaaS," or "fleet management sales," then those terms better be listed in your skills.

Be bold and specific here. Pick skills that directly align with how you solve problems—keywords your buyers would type into search, skills that match what you discuss in your headline, About section, and Experience. This consistency creates cohesion and drives higher search rankings.

- **Lead with the right three.** Pin your top three most relevant skills at the top of the list. These are ones LinkedIn highlights, people see first, and the most likely to get endorsed. They carry the most weight, so make them count.

- **Align your skills with your story.** If your About and Experience sections talk about solving complex problems, but your skills list reads like a software manual, you've got a disconnect.

- **Give endorsements to get endorsements.** It's a simple gesture, but it often sparks a chain reaction. You give a little credibility, you get some back. And the more endorsements you rack up on your top skills, the more weight they carry with profile viewers. When someone sees your top three skills backed by names they know, it de-risks you. It's social proof money can't buy.

Don't phone this in. The Skills section is one of the few places where the algorithm and the human eye meet. Use it to make yourself findable, credible, and clear.

> ## AI PRO TIP
>
> **Skill Prompt 1:** I work in the [industry] sector and specialize in [solution/role]. What are the most relevant LinkedIn skills and search keywords for someone in my position to get discovered by potential clients or employers?
>
> **Skill Prompt 2:** I'm a [job title] who sells [product/service] to [target audience/industry]. What are the most important hard and soft skills I should include on my LinkedIn profile to attract buyers and decision-makers in this space?

Step 15: Get Recommendations

Every great salesperson knows that what others say about you carries more weight than what you say about yourself.

LinkedIn recommendations are a referral and a five-star review rolled into one. In sales, nothing speaks louder than a client or colleague saying, "This person made a real impact." It's the ultimate de-risker.

The Recommendations You Give and Get Deliver Impact in Unexpected Ways

Allan, an account executive, had just wrapped a complex rollout with a major client. It was a tough project—tight timelines, multiple teams, a hundred moving parts. But one person kept it all glued together: Jen, the client's project manager.

She was a force. Clear communicator. Sharp operator. Always one step ahead. Because of her leadership, the project didn't just meet expectations—it launched three weeks early. Allan was so impressed, he wrote her a glowing recommendation on LinkedIn, spotlighting her strengths and the success they'd shared.

That single, kind gesture was paid back tenfold. A few months later, Allan got a message from one of Jen's connections. He'd seen the recommendation, checked Allan out, and wanted to talk about a project of his own. Just like that, a deal opened—not from a cold call, but from a public display of appreciation and proof of performance. That's the magic of LinkedIn recommendations.

Give to Get

The best way to get recommendations is to start giving them. Write sincere, specific, and story-driven recommendations for people you've worked with—especially clients and colleagues who brought out your best work. When you lift others up, two things happen: They're more likely to return the favor, and your name stays visible on their profiles.

Avoid vague praise. Instead, focus on real results and shared wins. What did you solve? What changed because of your work? Who benefited? For example:

Jen led a cross-functional team during our software rollout, keeping everyone aligned and on schedule. Her ability to drive collaboration helped us launch three weeks ahead of target. I'd work with her again in a heartbeat.

When you write a thoughtful recommendation for a client, it's not just a kind gesture—it's smart positioning. Your words

show up on their profile, increase your visibility to their network, reinforce your role as a trusted partner, and make your
client feel very important.

How to Ask for a Recommendation

The key to getting recommendations is to ask for them. When
asking, timing is everything. Ask right after a successful project
or milestone, when your impact is fresh in their mind. When
asking for a recommendation:

- **Be specific.** Don't just ask, "Can you write me a recommendation?" Tell them what you'd like them to focus on.
- **Explain why.** Let them know their words will help others
  understand the value you bring—and that their recommendation will live on your profile as a testimonial.
- **Make it easy.** Offer to provide a short draft they can tweak.
  This helps them get started and ensures the right story
  gets told.

*[Name], I've really enjoyed working with you on [specific
project or milestone].*

*I'm writing to ask if you'll be open to posting a short LinkedIn
recommendation about your experience working with me? It
will mean a lot, and it helps others see the kind of work I do
through the lens of people I've worked with.*

*If it's helpful, I'm happy to send over a quick draft you can edit
or use as a starting point if that makes things easier for you.*

Thanks again—it's been a pleasure collaborating with you!

Recommendations Are Living Proof That You Are Trustworthy

Recommendations are more than professional compliments. They're solid, visible evidence that you're someone worth trusting. In sales, trust is currency. Every recommendation on your profile chips away at skepticism and reinforces that you deliver real value to real people in the real world.

Don't wait for people to recommend you. Earn it. Ask for it. It's a strategic asset that works for you long after the deal is closed.

Your LinkedIn Profile Is a Runway to Higher Credibility and More Leads

You've just rebuilt your LinkedIn profile from the ground up. No more fluff. No more filler. Every section now works together to tell a single, powerful story—who you help, how you help, why you're worth talking to, and that you are low risk and trustworthy.

From your banner to your About section, your content to your credibility signals, you've created a scroll-stopping, trust-building, lead-generating digital presence that gives you an unfair advantage.

Here's the best part: while your competitors treat LinkedIn like a digital résumé, you're treating it like a launch pad for visibility, influence, and opportunity. Your personal brand is no longer an accident—it's a strategic sales weapon.

Differentiation, Thought Leadership, and Authority

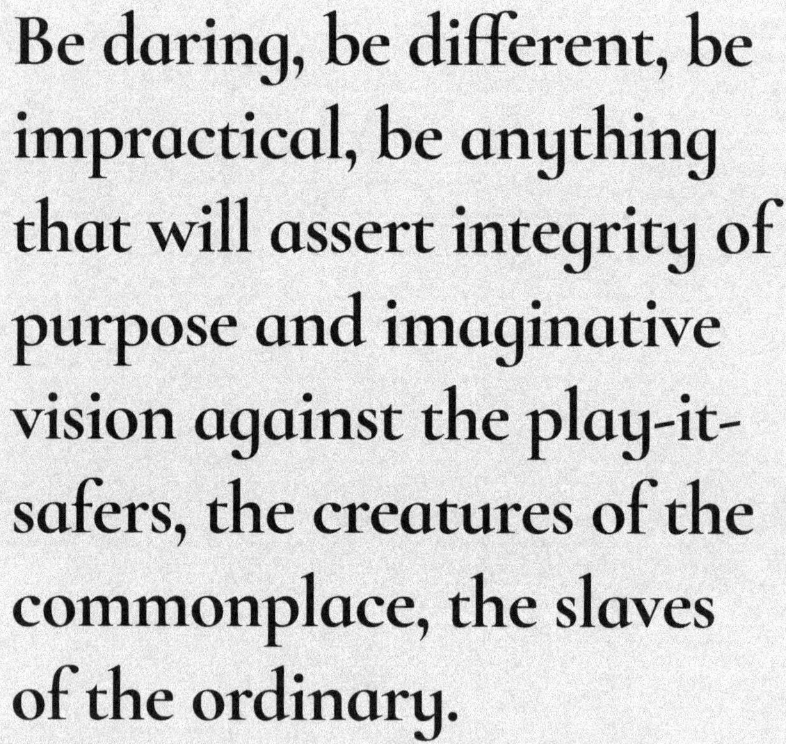

Be daring, be different, be impractical, be anything that will assert integrity of purpose and imaginative vision against the play-it-safers, the creatures of the commonplace, the slaves of the ordinary.

—*Cecil Beaton*

34

Authority in the Age of Transparency

We live in the age of transparency. The access to information is ubiquitous. Anyone with a screen and a few minutes can find practically anything they're looking for. And while that may sound like a good thing, more often than not it creates confusion for buyers.

When everything looks the same, when every vendor makes the same promises, when every blog sounds like it was written by ChatGPT on a deadline—buyers don't get clarity. They get paralysis.

Imagine a stakeholder researching software vendors. What do they find?

- Four companies claiming to solve the same problems
- Four websites that look nearly identical
- Four blogs with copycat articles

- Four identical landing pages offering four nearly identical white papers
- Four explainer videos full of jargon and buzzwords
- An AI-produced briefing on the pros and cons of each but no definitive answers or recommendations

They contact four account executives only for each account executive to roll in with a beautifully polished pitch deck, reciting the same generic messages, touting the same differentiators, and promising the same future state. Four meetings. Four smiling faces. Four pitches that all blur together.

Selling in an Ocean of Sameness

In this ocean of sameness, differentiating on the attributes of products, services, software, or price is more difficult than ever before. Yet far too many salespeople are merely walking, talking marketing brochures.

Buyers have become cynical and impatient with canned pitches. They want to engage in conversations with expert professionals who can actually help them. Therefore, in the age of transparency, the one true way to differentiate is through your personal brand and authority.

People Buy You

People aren't buying your product, service, or software. They are buying you—the person they believe can help them solve their problems. Strip away the tech. The decks. The features. The marketing brochures. And what's left? One human solving another human's problem. That's exactly what sales comes down to at its foundation.

Dr. Robert Cialdini, author of *Influence: The Psychology of Persuasion*, describes authority as one of the six fundamental levers of persuasion. When someone sees you as a credible expert, they're more likely to listen, trust, and follow your lead.

Studies in behavioral economics show that people are far more likely to take action when they perceive the source of the recommendation as credible and competent.

This is the real power of authority in sales. When you're seen as a trusted expert—someone who brings insight, context, and confidence to the conversation—your recommendations carry weight. Your advice doesn't feel like a pitch, but rather a path forward.

Building Authority

Authority isn't just what you know—it's how you communicate what you know. It's how you make others feel when they interact with you. Safe. Seen. Understood.

Building authority is about showing your work, sharing your perspective, and being visible in the right ways, to the right people, consistently over time. It's about positioning yourself as a trusted advisor worth listening to.

When you start capturing that insight and sharing it on LinkedIn, you position yourself as someone worth knowing. In a world flooded with sameness, authority is the signal that cuts through the noise. It gives your personal brand power, credibility, and magnetism.

Build your authority. Be the expert. And people will buy you.

35

Socially Surrounding Targeted Prospects with the Five S Framework

*T**he three primary objectives of slow prospecting are to:*

1. Attract prospects to you and generate hot inbound leads
2. Get warm introductions and referrals to target prospects
3. Improve the probability that you get more meetings with less resistance from outbound touches

Accomplishing these objectives requires surrounding your prospects with value—consistently showing up in their feeds through original content, curated insights, and meaningful engagement. This transforms you from another salesperson pitching into a trusted expert they want to hear from.

In the last chapter we discussed why your authority, presence, and credibility are key differentiators in a world of sameness and commoditization. Socially surrounding your target audience with content is how you engineer and operationalize that authority to improve prospecting outcomes.

The Five S Framework

The Five S framework is an intentional, strategic formula for systematically, socially surrounding your prospects so they come to know you, trust you, and view you as an expert authority in your field. The framework features:

1. Streaming
2. Sharing
3. Scrolling
4. Showing up
5. Searching

When executed consistently, this framework becomes a crucial link in your personal brand building tool kit that helps you build magnetic authority that attracts new pipeline opportunities and warms up the coldest of cold calls.

Streaming: Produce Content Your Prospects Consume

Streaming is how you insert yourself into your target ICP prospects' feed with relevant ideas, stories, and insights that they want to consume.

When you consistently post original, thought-provoking content, you position yourself as someone who understands the space, has a perspective, and is worth paying attention to.

This is where you start building familiarity at scale. It's where your prospects begin to recognize your voice and face, and associate you with credibility. On LinkedIn, if you're not consistently streaming content, you become invisible.

Sharing: Earn Reciprocity and Expand Reach

Sharing is where you become a maven. It positions you as the go-to resource for what matters right now in your space. When you share useful third-party content, relevant industry articles, or even your prospect's posts, you build goodwill and demonstrate that you're tuned into industry issues and trends.

The beautiful thing about sharing is that you don't have to be the original source. As the curator you get to add your thoughtful comments and gain authority by association.

As a bonus, when you thoughtfully amplify the voices of others (especially your prospects), you trigger the law of reciprocity. People notice. And they remember who elevated them. That's a powerful personal branding, multi-threading, and lead generation play.

Scrolling: Engineer Visibility in Their Feed

The LinkedIn experience is built around the home screen feed. When you and your prospects go to LinkedIn, it's the first thing you see.

The feed is crucial because it holds users on the platform as they scroll through it, looking for posts that interest them. What shows up is driven by LinkedIn's mysterious, ever-changing algorithm. But one thing we do know about the algorithm is that content engagement drives visibility in the feed.

Your ultimate goal is to stream and share content that both shows up in their feed and compels them to *stop their scroll*, click, and engage.

Searching: Optimize to Get Found

What you must never forget is that LinkedIn is a massive search engine that is indexed by other search engines. Optimizing for search is how you get found.

Your headline, profile summary, skills, featured content, and activity feed are all searchable assets that either help or hurt your chances of showing up.

Your objective is to be found when buyers go looking for help with the problems they solve. For this reason you must always be disciplined with and focused on optimizing your profile and everything you post on LinkedIn for search.

Showing Up: Be Present Where It Matters

Most salespeople lurk. They scroll silently and wonder why nothing happens.

Showing up is about active participation, not passive scrolling. Move beyond quick likes to meaningful engagement through thoughtful comments and genuine conversation. Strategically engage with your prospects, network, and industry leaders. Turn every comment on your posts into an opportunity for deeper dialogue.

Showing up gives you an advantage because when you're present, visible, and generous with your attention, people start to feel like they know you (familiarity). And when they know you, they trust you.

A Steady Drumbeat of Credibility

The Five S's are the key to surrounding your prospects with a steady drumbeat of credibility and staying top-of-mind without being in their face.

This is how you prospect without prospecting, earn authority and become the safe choice, cross the familiarity threshold, and separate yourself in a sea of sameness. And the moment they need help solving a problem, you're already there.

36

Streaming: Creating and Posting Original Content That Builds Your Authority

The best analogy to help you step into the role of a streamer is to think of LinkedIn as if it's the "Netflix of Business." Your stream of content is just one show on this vast media network. Your objective is to produce enough consistently relevant content to hook your audience and keep them tuning into you.

To keep your audience engaged, your content stream needs a predictable cadence and rhythm. This is how you go from what Brynne calls "random acts of social" to a must-watch thought leader.

The key to an effective LinkedIn content strategy is not trying to be everything to everyone. You're carving out a niche channel that speaks directly to your target prospects and their challenges.

Posting Original Content Gains More Visibility

Creating and publishing original content on LinkedIn is the lynchpin in your slow prospecting strategy. It builds your personal brand recognition and helps you become the go-to resource for your prospects—someone they trust, respect, and turn to when they're ready to buy.

Importantly, the LinkedIn algorithms place greater emphasis on original, native content, which means your stream is more likely to be seen, commented on and shared—giving you even greater visibility to your target ICP prospects.

This Is Hard Work

Let's keep this real though. Becoming a consistent streamer of original content on LinkedIn is hard freaking work. You cannot be on again, off again, and be effective.

A big challenge is the ocean of content flooding the LinkedIn stream. Most of it has a shelf life of a few hours at most. Therefore, to break through and earn eyeballs, you must be on your game with new, relevant content, spanning different formats, every single day.

It's a grind. There will be days when you are absolutely sick of it. We've been doing it for years so we know this firsthand that keeping up a steady daily cadence of new, original content can be exhausting.

An effective content streaming strategy requires you to:

- Develop a content streaming plan.
- Be a creative thinker, always on the lookout for new ideas and new angles on old ideas.

- Research, read, and stay ahead of industry trends. This means blocking time daily for professional reading and listening to podcasts and audiobooks.
- Keep up with the latest content format trends and changes in the LinkedIn algorithm.
- Get out of your comfort zone, get vulnerable, and put yourself out there.
- Be resilient and keep going while you endure the gut-wrenching emotions that occur when you get hammered with negative comments or no one shows up to like, comment, or share on a post you put your whole heart into.
- Have the regimented discipline to consistently produce and post new content.

The more your audience engages with your content, the more the algorithm works in your favor, the more content gets recommended, your face shows up in feeds, and you start moving across the familiarity threshold.

Consistency Matters

A post here and a like there, randomly and infrequently is like whispering into a hurricane and expecting your voice to be heard. Skip too many episodes, and your audience will forget you. Show up inconsistently and your content gets buried.

That's why consistency matters more than brilliance or perfection. To be consistent, you must be disciplined and push through the desire to take a day off.

A best practice is to post original content two to three days per week and share curated content on other days. We're fans of posting original content on Tuesdays, Wednesdays, and Thursdays. Studies from social media platforms, including

SproutSocial and Buffer, have shown these days yield the best engagement.

There is debate about the best timing for your posts. The consensus from multiple sources seems to coalesce around posting from 10 a.m. to 1 p.m. But because you are in sales and not making your living as a social media influencer, let's dispense with that.

Instead of attempting to time your posts, just post first thing early each morning (this is what Jeb does). This gives your content an entire day to work for you and gets this activity out of the way before you are consumed by your sales day—making it more likely that you will not forget.

Scheduling Posts

If you find maintaining a daily posting cadence challenging, consider scheduling your posts in batches. Although the LinkedIn algorithm is known to punish scheduled posts, scheduling can help you maintain a steady stream of content. This is easy to do using the scheduler built right into LinkedIn:

1. Create a post as you normally would.
2. Click or tap the clock icon to access scheduling options.
3. Select a date and time for your post.
4. Click "Next" to proceed.
5. Click or tap "Schedule" to finalize the process.

In addition, tools like Buffer, Hootsuite, SproutSocial, and HubSpot offer robust options for managing and scheduling posts in advance.

Post Types

Leveraging a variety of post formats keeps your content fresh and engaging. People consume information differently—some prefer reading articles, while others gravitate toward visuals or interactive posts. LinkedIn offers multiple formats that cater to different preferences and can elicit unique responses from your audience:

- **Text posts:** Short, punchy, story-driven insights. Great for engagement and easy to create.
- **LinkedIn articles:** Searchable, longer, deeper dives that help establish authority and thought leadership.
- **Videos:** Let them see your face, hear your tone, feel your energy. Video creates intimacy and is an effective way to tell your story. Also a great way to drop short, impactful clips from podcasts, webinars, presentations, and speeches.
- **Single images:** The original interest grabber and scroll stopper on text posts.
- **Infographics and carousels:** Visual storytelling that breaks down complex ideas.
- **Polls:** Quick hits of interaction. Invites opinions. Sparks curiosity.
- **LinkedIn livestreams:** Interact in real time with your audience. Great for Q&A, training, or insights.

Some posts build awareness. Some deepen trust. Some drive conversations. For instance, a well-crafted video can convey emotion and urgency, while a detailed article allows for a deep dive into complex topics.

The key is to mix your content intentionally. You don't have to use every type every week—but you should rotate, experiment, and test what appeals best to your audience.

Planning

Just like any successful sales activity, you need to have a plan in place. Otherwise you'll wake up each morning and either randomly post anything you can come up with or skip the day altogether because developing an original idea in the spur of the moment is too mentally challenging.

As a best practice, it's preferable to plan your original content cadence in advance either weekly or monthly. For example, Jeb and his team at Sales Gravy, plan a content series around a theme each month and build it into a formal calendar.

A content series is a sequence of related content pieces that explore a specific topic in-depth.

1. Choose a theme that is relevant and valuable to your target audience and broad enough to allow for multiple pieces of content.
2. Outline the topics for each content piece and ensure they flow logically and build on each other.
3. Set a schedule for releasing each piece of content.

If you need help developing ideas and a content strategy, tap into AI. It's a great partner for building your LinkedIn content streaming plan.

AI PRO TIP

Content Strategy Prompt: I want to build a LinkedIn content strategy with three original posts per week—on Monday, Tuesday, and Thursday—designed to resonate with [insert your ICP]. Each month will have a central theme. For this month, the theme is [insert theme].

Please build a four-week posting plan that includes:

- One post per week that's text-based (story, insight, perspective, or lesson)
- One post per week that includes a media element (video, carousel, infographic, poll, etc.)

(Continued)

(*Continued*)

- One post per week that drives engagement or conversation (asks a question, invites comments, shares a point of view)
- A content angle or message that ties back to the monthly theme
- Suggested post titles or headlines
- Short briefs or outlines for each post
- AI prompts I can use to draft each post faster

Make sure this plan is designed for building authority, thought leadership, and trust with my audience. Keep it consistent with my voice and style: direct, smart, value-driven, and conversation-starting.

Block Time for Dedicated Focus on Creating Original Content

Creating original content is time consuming. That's why so many salespeople skip it. It is a lot easier, though, when you block dedicated time for it and work from a content streaming plan.

A plan and strategy—monthly themes, weekly topics, targeted formats—eliminates the mental friction and anxiety of trying to figure out what to post each day.

Block at least two hours per week—outside of the golden hours—for uninterrupted creative time. Protect this block like you protect your prospecting window.

Tools That Make Content Creation Easier

You'll move faster and more confidently when you leverage modern content creation tools. These tools cut down production time, boost quality, and keep you from reinventing the wheel every week. The chart shows some of our favorites.

Tool	Category	Primary Use
Canva	Design	Create infographics, carousels, banners, and branded images.
Opus.pro	Video editing	Turn long-form videos into short, snackable clips.
ChatGPT/Claude/ Jasper/Gemini/ MS Co-Pilot	AI writing, image, and content creation	Brainstorm, refine messaging, and convert notes into posts, images, guides, and videos.
Notebook LM	AI content builder	Generate FAQs, quizzes, polls, and podcasts.
Grammarly/ Hemingway Editor	Editing	Improve grammar, clarity, and writing quality.
Descript	Audio/video editing	Edit video/audio like a doc; remove filler and transcribe.
Screen Pal/ Tella/Loom	Video recording	Record webcam video insights or commentary.
Notion/Evernote/ Apple Notes	Note taking	Capture ideas, phrases, and customer insights.
Trello/ Airtable/ClickUp	Planning	Track themes, post status, and maintain visibility.
Fathom	Meeting intelligence	Transcribes and summarizes Zoom calls for post ideas.
Bubbles	Async video	Record screen shares or async thoughts as shareable clips.
Brevity	Summarization	Convert meetings into quote cards and visual highlights.
SwipeWell	Inspiration	Save inspiring posts/headlines as swipe files.
Zubtitle	Video captioning	Add captions and headlines to videos for silent scrolling.
Headliner	Audiogram creation	Create short audio-visual posts from longer audio.

(Continued)

(*Continued*)

Tool	Category	Primary Use
Feedly	Content curation	Follow trends and curate industry news for commentary.
SparkToro	Audience intelligence	Identify what your ICP reads, watches, and shares.
VideoLeap	Video editor	Powerful, all-in-one mobile video editing App (Jeb's favorite).

The key to getting started with any of these tools is to sign up for the free version and start experimenting until you find the ones that are right for you.

We've named just a handful of the tools available. There are many more out there that can elevate your LinkedIn content streaming game. Take a moment now, do an online search, or better yet, ask your AI assistant to help you.

37

Sharing: Building Authority Through Content Curation

If original content is the fuel that powers building and elevating your personal brand, curation is your secret weapon for staying visible and relevant with far less effort. You don't need to start from scratch and craft a Pulitzer-worthy post every day to maintain a steady stream of content. Sometimes the smartest move is putting your stamp on someone else's voice.

Curation is finding content published by others and sharing it while adding your own spin. This could mean giving a brief summary, pulling out a thought-provoking quote, or adding your perspective.

Reposting insightful content from experts, prospects, customers, and peers signals that you're plugged in and positions you as a maven, connector, and conversation catalyst.

The beautiful thing about content curation is, even though you didn't produce the content, when you repost with your comments and perspective, some of the authority rubs off on you.

Be Aware and Know Your Space

You need to be aware of what is happening in your industry—trends, competitors, movers and shakers. Have your eyes and ears open, pay attention to what is going on around you, and consume industry-specific media.

When you come across content that resonates with your audience, ask yourself:

- Why is this important right now?
- Who in my network would benefit from seeing this?
- What unique perspective can I add?

That last question matters. A lot. When you curate content, you're not just reposting—you're reframing. You're connecting the dots and positioning yourself as a subject matter expert.

Tap into the Right Sources

To curate valuable content, you need a steady flow of fresh ideas, insights, and industry updates. That means knowing where to look and building systems that bring that content to you:

- Pull from your own company blog, podcast, and YouTube channel.
- Subscribe to industry blogs and trade publications.
- Follow the thought leaders and experts who are shaping the dialogue in your industry.

- Grab relevant articles from news sources like *The Wall Street Journal* or *Bloomberg*.

- Share posts from your prospects, customers, and professional network.

- Use tools like Feedly or SparkToro to discover trending content in your industry niche.

- Set up Google alerts to email you when new content in your niche is published.

A systematic approach ends the panic of "what should I post today?" and transforms content curation from an overwhelming task into a powerful competitive weapon.

The FIRE Method

Follow the FIRE method, you shift content curation into the realm of closer content creation by pulling key lessons from the original content, linking the threads, and adding your own perspective:

- **Frame:** Open by framing the original content. In one or two sentences, set the context so your audience knows exactly why it matters and why it's worth their time.

- **Insight:** Add your unique insight. Highlight key lessons, connect the dots, and share your perspective to deepen understanding. (This requires that you take the time to fully understand what you're sharing.)

- **Relate:** Relate the content back to your audience's situation. Tie it to their goals, challenges, or interests to make it more personal and relevant.

- **Evoke:** Evoke responses and conversation by asking a compelling question that invites comments and deeper dialogue.

Tag the original author or source with an @mention. This brings their attention to your post, encourages them to engage with a comment, and encourages reciprocity.

AI PRO TIP

Content Curation Prompt: I need help with reposting content on LinkedIn with my thoughts. I want to use the LinkedIn Content FIRE method:

Frame: Open by framing the original content. In one or two sentences, set the context so your audience knows exactly why it matters and why it's worth their time.

Insight: Add your unique insight. Highlight key lessons, connect the dots, and share your perspective to deepen understanding.

Relate: Relate the content back to your audience's situation. Tie it to their goals, challenges, or interests to make it more personal and relevant.

Evoke: Evoke responses and conversation by asking a compelling question that invites comments and deeper dialogue.

This is what I want to repost using the FIRE method [insert post/article/transcript/video].

I also want you to pull a thought-provoking quote from the content that I can use to create an image for my repost.

(Note: Use **Canva** to put this quote into an eye-catching graphic for extra visual pop.)

This is the original post:

Dennis J Walker Jr · 1st
Benefits Consultant
Book an appointment
2d · 🌐

Jeb Blount regularly states that you can't be delisional about your pipe, your prospects, your efforts, etc and be successful as a salesperson.

This week one of the larger deals in my pipe definitely didn't progress the way I wanted- and it turns out one of the executives is what I call a "deal enemy" - he was actively working against me and my team.

The last two meetings I've had with him tipped me off this could be the case; this week we had an incident that indicated he was actively working against us.

Because my pipe is full?

I can walk away from this (probably very bad) deal at a dysfunctional company and not worry about hitting my sales goal.

With their current leadership, they'll be a terrible client.

Helping them will be painful.

And I know I can help them with creativity, doing things differently, and giving them a lot of what they want and have at better pricing and higher quality.

But I'm not freaking out.

Because I have 15 other prospects, three that are advancing well, and about a dozen additional companies with buying windows later this year or early next.

Go prospect. Go set appointments. It's amazing what happens when you get on the phone and walk in doors.

This is Claude's response:

FRAME: Dennis J Walker just shared a powerful reminder about why a robust sales pipeline isn't just about numbers—it's about freedom and strategic decision-making. His recent experience with a "deal enemy" perfectly illustrates why prospecting discipline pays dividends beyond just hitting quota.

(Continued)

(*Continued*)

> **INSIGHT:** What strikes me most about Dennis's story is the psychological shift that happens when you're prospecting from abundance versus scarcity. When your pipeline is thin, every prospect feels like life or death, leading to poor decisions and desperate behavior. But when you're consistently filling your funnel, you gain something invaluable: the power to walk away from bad-fit clients. This isn't just about sales metrics—it's about protecting your energy, reputation, and long-term success. The best salespeople understand that not every deal is worth winning.
>
> **RELATE:** How many of us have stayed in toxic sales situations simply because we didn't have better options lined up? Whether you're in sales, consulting, or running your own business, this principle applies universally. A strong pipeline gives you negotiating power, helps you maintain your standards, and allows you to focus on clients who truly value what you bring to the table.
>
> **EVOKE:** What's the worst "deal enemy" situation you've encountered, and how did having (or not having) other options influence your decision to stay or walk away?
>
> **THOUGHT-PROVOKING QUOTE FOR IMAGE:** *"It's amazing what happens when you get on the phone and walk in doors."*

Feeding the Stream

You cannot create enough original content to feed the stream. That's the reality. Curation is how you stay relevant in between original posts without burning yourself out. So don't just scroll past great content. Curate it. Shape it. Share it. And use it to open conversations that create pipeline opportunities.

38

Stop the Scroll: Creative Inspiration for Content That Connects

In today's crowded LinkedIn feed, attention is the ultimate currency. You can craft the smartest post and share the sharpest insight, but none of it matters if you can't get someone to stop scrolling long enough to notice. That's the first battle you have to win: earning just a fraction of a second of attention—enough to pull the reader out of autopilot and into your content stream.

The Five Elements of Magnetic Content That Stops the Scroll

When posting to your LinkedIn stream, you'll be amazed at how often little things get big results. Sometimes the stickiest post is a quick insight, useful visual, or even a picture of you with a new customer after closing the sale.

Let go of perfection and give yourself permission to be creative and try different ideas. If you miss the mark, no worries, LinkedIn posts have a very short shelf life.

As you invest time into building your content stream, use the LinkedIn analytics feature built right into each of your posts to dial into the formats and content that resonate most with your target audience (Figure 38.1).

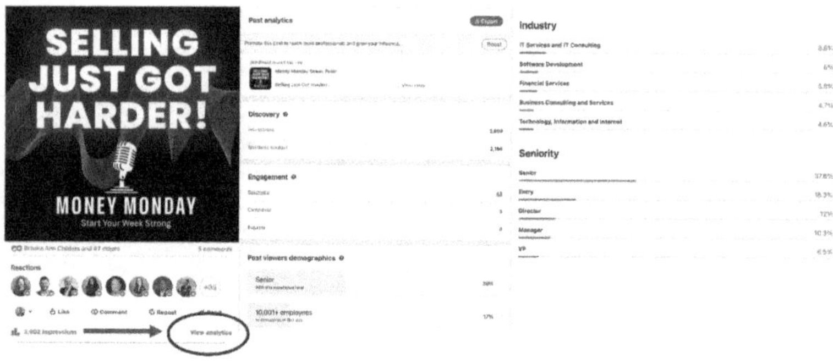

Figure 38.1 LinkedIn post analytics.

You also get detailed information about who is consuming your content, their industries, and companies. With this information, you can identify content themes and formats that generate the most engagement from your target ICP audience.

To make your content stand out, and stop the scroll aim to hit these five marks:

1. **Resonate with your audience:** Your content should reflect your target audience's reality—pain, problems, aspirations, and goals. When people see themselves in your post, they stop scrolling.

2. **Create curiosity:** Your hook is your headline. Ask a bold
   question. Share an unexpected insight. Drop a stat that
   stops the scroll. Curiosity earns clicks.

3. **Teach something new:** Give them something they can use.
   A tip. A process. A "how-to." A way to see something
   differently. Teaching builds trust and positions you as
   an expert.

4. **Make them think:** Challenge the status quo. Offer a contrarian
   point of view. Reframe the conversation. When you shift
   perspectives, you create space for discussion.

5. **Move them from scroller to engager:** Don't just
   broadcast—invite engagement. Ask questions.
   Encourage replies. Activate conversations.

When your content hits these five marks, it will connect, stop
the scroll, and leave your prospects hungry for more.

Creative Inspiration Is All Around You

Finding inspiration for what to post may seem daunting at first
but it isn't as hard as it seems once you open your mind and start
looking around you. There are ideas everywhere. The key is
intentional awareness and letting go of perfectionism so that
creative thinking becomes a habit rather than a hurdle.

The secret is simply stepping into the shoes of your target
ICP and considering their pain points, questions, problems,
interests, what makes them feel understood, and what grabs
their attention.

Through this lens, don't wait for inspiration to hit you. Hunt
for it, everywhere: Real conversations. Common objections.
Trends in your industry. Customer stories. Your story. Human
interest. Authenticity. These are the raw materials of powerful
content that stops the scroll.

Video Content

LinkedIn's data shows that videos get five times more engagement than standard posts. Consider creating:

- Short explainer videos offering industry insights or practical tips
- Behind-the-scenes content that humanizes your brand
- Day-in-the-life videos showing your work processes
- Interview highlights that showcase your expertise or industry connections
- Sales recaps (summarizing client meetings while keeping details anonymous)
- Client testimonials (with permission)
- "Man-on-the-street" interviews gathering opinions and viewpoints
- Quick clips from industry speakers or events
- Product demonstrations
- Personal updates about accomplishments or partnerships
- Clips from webinars, events, podcasts, and interviews

The beautiful thing about video content is that it's easy to create because you always have a camera in your hand. And with AI-powered editing tools you can build highly engaging, professional video content on the fly. It's like having a full production crew in your back pocket. Just point, shoot, edit, and post.

Text Posts

Use storytelling techniques to connect with your audience emotionally and drive engagement in text posts:

- **Commentary on industry trends:** Add your perspective to the news. Let your audience know how it impacts them.

- **Behind-the-scenes stories:** Share what you're working on. Show the process, not just the result.
- **Client FAQs:** Turn common questions into content. If someone asked the question, someone else is thinking it.
- **Mini how-tos or quick tips:** Actionable advice helps your audience solve a small problem quickly.
- **Lessons from the field:** Share what you learned from a win, loss, or other life experiences. Authenticity absolutely resonates.
- **Repurposed conversations:** Did you make a great point on a call? That's a post.
- **Book or podcast reactions:** What did you read or hear that challenged your thinking?

There are two types of text-based posts to consider: long-form and short-form.

Long-Form Text Posts

These are two- to three-paragraph, single-topic text posts of 175 words or less, with no outbound links. Long-form is an excellent way to pull additional content from original articles. AI can do this for you in a jiffy. Just paste your article into ChatGPT, Claude, or Gemini and prompt it to give you 175-word summaries.

Short-Form Text Posts

These are easy-to-consume posts of 280 characters or fewer that can garner a lot of attention when you have the right content. AI can quickly repurpose long-form content into short posts. Just paste an article, transcript, or media file into your AI assistant and prompt: *Please give me five short social media posts from this content.* In a matter of seconds you'll be in business.

Visual Content

Incorporate eye-catching graphics, infographics, and images to complement your text. Visuals enhance engagement and communicate complex ideas more effectively, making your content more shareable and appealing. This type of visual content is super easy to build in Canva. Consider creating:

- Trend or data infographics
- Process visualizations
- "How-to" graphics
- Behind-the-scenes images
- Team photos or company events
- Quotes and memes

When posting multiple images, be strategic about the format. LinkedIn offers both collage and carousel displays—collages show all images simultaneously, while carousels allow users to swipe through content and provide a more interactive experience (to create a carousel, upload your images as a PDF).

LinkedIn Articles

When you need to delve deeper into a topic or share a longer, in-depth piece of content, publish an article. Articles are the perfect medium for positioning yourself as an authority.

Articles are longer lasting than regular posts, are pinned to your profile, and improve your visibility in search both within LinkedIn and on Google, Bing, and AI search engines.

To write an article, you'll need to click the "Write an article" icon. You'll get blog-style editing tools that allow you to include a large headline, a separate section for body copy, and embed rich media, including links, videos, and images.

Polls for Prospecting Intel

Polls create quick interaction points, provide valuable insight into audience preferences or industry trends, and foster a sense of community among your connections. They give your audience a reason to stop scrolling, think, and respond.

A well-crafted poll invites engagement, reveals pain points, and helps you understand what matters to your audience right now. The keys to creating scroll-stopping polls include:

- **Relevant:** Ask about challenges your prospects face in their daily work.
- **Timely:** Tie polls to current events, seasonal shifts, or industry changes.
- **Punchy:** Keep questions concise and options easy to understand.
- **Open the door to conversation:** Use comments to dig deeper. "Curious—what's behind your vote?"

Here are a few poll types to rotate into your content stream:

- **Pain points and challenges:** What's the biggest challenge you're facing with [topic] right now?
- **Preference testing:** If you could only focus on one area for Q4, what would it be?
- **Stakeholder persona research:** When evaluating new tech, who do you involve first?
- **Trend tapping:** In the next 12 months, what's the one trait that will separate top companies in [industry].
- **Humor:** Be honest. How often do you really read the onboarding playbook?

Think of your polls as prospecting intel. The comment section can be a goldmine for follow-up. When someone votes or comments, you now have a context-aware reason to reach out. "Hey, I noticed you voted on my poll about [X]—curious to hear more about how you're approaching it."

Go Live

If content is how you earn visibility, then going live on LinkedIn is how you turn visibility into instant connection. It's raw, human, and unfiltered—which is exactly why it works.

LinkedIn Live is the best way to stop the scroll and turn your stream into a real-time, two way conversation because you can respond to questions live and turn viewers into participants.

It's important to note that you don't need a huge audience. You need the right audience. Here are a few formats that work:

- Go live once a week and break down something you learned from a recent deal, call, meeting or by solving a customer problem. Keep it short (10–15 minutes) and actionable: "Here's a question I asked on a discovery call this week that unlocked an interesting conversation."
- Pick a question or objection you hear all the time and share why it is valid and how you answer it.

- Run a 15-minute live tutorial on a topic your customers or prospects care about that can make their life easier.
- React to news, trends, or big shifts in your industry. Offer your POV in real time: "Here's what this means for leaders in [industry] with distributed teams . . ."
- Interview a happy client. Let them tell the story of the problem you solved, and your solution becomes the hero behind the scenes.
- Collect common questions about your product, service, or software and answer them live.
- Co-host with someone from marketing, product, or customer success. Talk about what you're seeing in the field and how it connects to your company's strategy.

Tips for Successful Live Sessions

- **Promote early:** Announce your live session at least 48 hours in advance. Tease the topic, tag people and build curiosity.
- **Time it well:** Mid-morning or early afternoon usually perform best. Avoid Fridays unless it's casual or community-focused.
- **Engage in real time:** Shout out commenters. Take questions. Let your audience shape the session.
- **Keep it tight:** Shorter sessions (under 30 minutes) perform better and are easier to repurpose.
- **Record and repurpose:** Share key takeaways. Chop the replay into 30–90 second clips (use Opus.pro) and turn the transcript into an article or a series of posts.

As a bonus, the replay remains available on your profile under the Events tab, extending the content's reach, allowing those who missed the live broadcast to benefit from your insights, and helping your search results.

Leveraging AI for Content Inspiration

AI can quickly analyze current trends in your industry by processing information from recent articles, research papers, and popular discussions. Use it to identify what topics are gaining traction in your field or to break through creator's block.

It can also help you brainstorm different angles or perspectives on trending topics. For example, if a particular technology is trending, AI can help generate content ideas that cover its implications, future developments, or case studies from businesses that have adopted it.

Here are a few AI prompts to get you started:

- "I am a [role] selling [product, service, software] to [target ICP]. I primarily solve [problems and challenges]. I'm putting together a LinkedIn content strategy and need help brainstorming ideas that will engage my target ICP."
- "What are the top five trends impacting this [industry]. Please cite sources and provide links."
- "Write a LinkedIn post about [pain point] that shares a personal story and ends with a call to comment."
- "Turn this bullet point list into a short post with a strong hook: [paste bullets]."
- "Suggest five headlines for a post about [insert topic]."
- "Write a 200-word LinkedIn post using this quote as the theme: [paste quote]."
- "Generate a catchy introduction for a post about [insert topic here]." This can help you formulate engaging content that captures attention and drives interaction.
- "I'm looking for original full length LinkedIn article ideas for [target ICP] that has this [challenge]. Please give me 10 titles and ask me to choose the one I want. Then write the content in a way that leads to [my solution] but is not pitchy.

The content should have a hook, insights that create aha moments, and a CTA."

- Paste a link to an article you'd like summarized for LinkedIn. Then prompt: "Recap this article in under 500 characters, including the author, publication, a direct quote, and a plain-text link with a 'Read full post' line. Also write a CTA inviting comments. Add three relevant hashtags."

Stories Stop the Scroll

When Brynne marked a major milestone—10 years cancer-free—she had learned the value of resilience, courage, and a deep gratitude for life and relationships.

When she was first diagnosed with breast cancer, everything stopped. The weight of the news was crushing. With four-year-old twin boys at home, she feared the moments she might miss.

In the middle of that fear, Brynne began recording video messages for her sons—capturing her values, hopes, and love. What began as a personal archive became much more.

When she eventually shared her story publicly, the response surprised her. People reached out. They related to her. They were moved. Her vulnerability created space for others to open up, and her story became a bridge—not just to empathy, but to trust and emotional connection.

That experience reshaped how Brynne approached both life and business. She learned that authentic storytelling allows people to see you not only as a sales professional but as an authentic human. And in the world of sameness and commoditization, that can make all the difference.

Today, storytelling remains at the heart of Brynne's personal brand. By sharing real experiences with courage and clarity, she continues to initiate conversations, foster community, and remind others that their stories matter, too.

Sometimes, because you are so close to it, it can be difficult to clearly articulate your story. This is where AI can give you a hand.

Prompt 1: Start with just recording your story in your own words. Then copy the transcript. (There are lots of ways to do this, including voice-to-text functions in MS Word and Google Docs, devices like Plaud, Zoom, Teams, or the voice memo app on your phone. Next, prompt your AI: Please help me write a compelling story for a LinkedIn post. I want you to use this framework:

Hook: Start with an intriguing hook that grabs my audience by their heart strings and pulls them in.
Struggle: Show my vulnerability and describe the struggle I faced in human terms that people can relate to in their own lives.
Breakthrough: Describe my breakthrough moment and what it felt like to overcome my challenges.
Lesson: Land the plane by offering the takeaways and lessons learned from my experience.

Prompt 2: You are a reporter for a magazine seeking to uncover a human-interest story that ends with lessons for your readers. I want you to interview me about my experience of getting fired from by dream job and then rising from the ashes using the HSBL story framework.

Hook: Start with an intriguing hook that grabs my audience by their heart strings and pulls them in.

> **Struggle:** Show my vulnerability and describe the struggle I faced in human terms that people can relate to in their own lives.
>
> **Breakthrough:** Describe my breakthrough moment and what it felt like to overcome my challenges.
>
> **Lesson:** Land the plane by offering the takeaways and lessons learned from my experience.
>
> Ask me one question at a time until you have all the information you need to craft a compelling story about my experience. Then write the story using the HSBL framework.

Your story is a crucial part of your personal brand. It allows you to connect on a human level, demonstrate authentic vulnerability, and makes you more memorable.

It's Really About Understanding Your Audience

Creating engaging LinkedIn content that stops the scroll is first and foremost about understanding your audience. By focusing on resonance, curiosity, education, perspective shifts, and engagement—while diversifying your content types and weaving in your story—you'll build a content stream that not only captures attention but converts interest into meaningful engagement and pipeline opportunities.

39

Search and
the LinkedIn Algorithm

Everything you do on LinkedIn should be done with discoverability in mind because in our digital-first world, if people can't find you, you don't exist.

Under the hood, LinkedIn runs on a sophisticated search algorithm. Your prospects use it every day—looking for vendors, experts, collaborators, and insights.

If your LinkedIn profile isn't optimized to be discovered when your ideal customer is actively looking, you're losing pipeline opportunities. If your content isn't visible in your target audience's feed, you're not just invisible—you're irrelevant.

The Two Algorithms at Play

LinkedIn runs on two powerful algorithms:

1. **Search:** This drives what shows up in the LinkedIn search
   bar. It's relevance-based, just like Google. It indexes your
   headline, About section, job titles, skills, hashtags, and even
   the text in your posts.
2. **Feed:** This determines what shows up in users' home feeds.
   It's engagement-driven, built to reward relevance, consistency,
   and time-on-post.

To win on LinkedIn, you must optimize for both. The objective
is straightforward: Make it easy for people to find you.

But before we move forward, it's important to note that the
search algorithm is always changing. You must stay current on
those changes and make regular adjustments to optimize
for search.

Know What You Want to Be Found For

Start by identifying which keywords and phrases best represent
your expertise—and make sure you're optimized for them.
Consider these questions:

- What would my ideal buyer type into the search bar if they
  were looking for someone like me?
- What words describe the solution I offer? The problems
  I solve?
- What role do I want to be known for in my industry?

Write these phrases down. These are your strategic keywords
and phrases.

Use Strategic Keywords and Phrases in the Right Places

Once you know your keywords, place them in the highest-impact zones:

- **Headline:** This is your billboard. Include both your function and the problems you solve.

- **About section:** Front-load this with your keywords. Write like a human, but think like a search engine.

- **Job titles:** Don't just write "Account Executive." Add context. Try: "Sr. Account Executive | Workforce Management Software for Distributed Teams."

- **Skills:** Add your top 10–15 skills that relate to your ICP's search behavior.

- **Posts, articles, and live:** Sprinkle in your keywords naturally across your content, especially in the first two to three lines.

- **Avoid gratuitous keyword stuffing:** Aim to use your core keywords three to five times across your profile— authentically and naturally.

- **Alt tags on images:** Add your keywords and phrases in different combinations as the alt tag on any image you post.

AI PRO TIP

Try a prompt like this to get started with keywords: Based on my job as a [insert title], who sells [insert product or service] to [insert ICP], generate a list of 20 strategic keywords and phrases that my prospects might search on LinkedIn to find someone like me. Then help me rewrite my LinkedIn headline and About section using those keywords in a way that sounds natural and compelling without keyword stuffing.

Engineering the LinkedIn Algorithm

At its core, the LinkedIn algorithm curates and delivers content that is most relevant to its users based on their interests, connections, and engagement history. Understanding how this algorithm works is vital for being visible to your network and targeting ICPs as they scroll through their feed.

Although constantly changing what it prioritizes, at its core the LinkedIn algorithm prioritizes content based on engagement, relevance, diversity, and consistency.[1] Here are the essential drivers:

- The first 90 minutes after posting are critical. The more likes, comments, shares you get in this window, the more your post will gain visibility.
- Reply to comments quickly to boost visibility and give your post momentum in the feed stream.
- Comments carry more weight than reactions. When your posts encourage longer comments, you move up in the algorithm.
- The more time people spend on your post, the more visibility it gains. Use spacing for readability and utilize carousels and videos to keep people on your posts longer.
- The more consistently you post, the more the algorithm rewards you. This does not mean that you need to make 10 posts a day. One good post daily keeps you consistent without becoming overwhelming.
- Posts that include a link to an outside resource are penalized by the algorithm. LinkedIn wants to keep people on its platform. Use these post types strategically and sparingly.

---

[1] For more extensive information on the LinkedIn Algorithm, see Richard van der Blom's Algorithm InSights report.

- Use hashtags strategically. Choose three to five per post. Mix niche-specific (#HRComplianceTools) with broader ones (#WorkforceManagement).

- To improve search, use a branded hashtag on every post. For example, Jeb uses #SellMore and Brynne #SSLInsights

- Mentioning individuals in your LinkedIn posts can boost visibility, but too many mentions, especially of those not directly relevant, can appear as spam and penalize you.

- Purely AI-generated content and comments are punished. Avoid straight copy/paste. Edit and humanize all AI-generated copy.

- Commenting on others' posts increases your visibility. Engaging with 10–20 accounts each day can boost profile views by 50 percent and increase followers by 10 percent.

Visibility Is Engineered

Visibility is not a fluke. It's engineered. The LinkedIn algorithm rewards intentionality, consistency, and relevance. Every line in your profile, every phrase in your content, and every comment you leave is an opportunity to be seen and discovered.

Take immediate ownership of your discoverability. Because when the right people find you at the right time, prospecting and pipeline building gets infinitely easier.

40

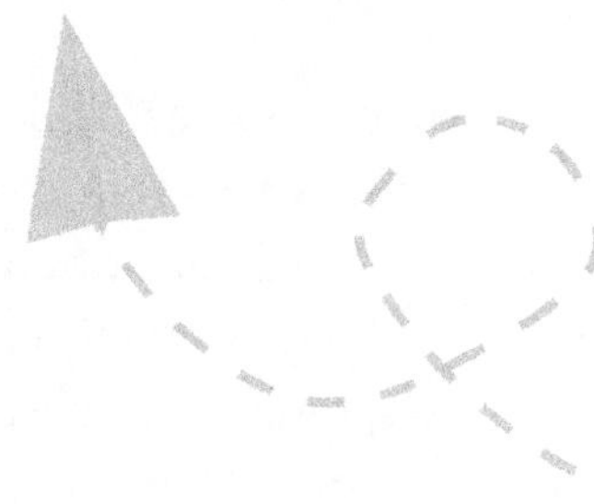

Showing Up in Comments and Conversation

It's tempting to believe that LinkedIn success comes from creating one brilliant post after another. But the truth is, that's only half the game. You can't just broadcast.

To build visibility and goodwill and generate inbound leads, you must show up in comments and conversations. This is where the real LinkedIn magic happens. Through interaction, you make others feel seen and important, keep your name top of mind, and cement authority and familiarity.

Practice the 10:1 Method

The LinkedIn search algorithm rewards commenters. There is even evidence that when you actively comment on others' posts, your original posts get even more visibility. Comments are so important that LinkedIn even gives you stats on how many impressions your comments received.

There's something powerful about moving from passive lurking to actively engaging. That shift—from reading to responding, from watching to contributing—is foundational to building a voice and a presence that people remember. For this reason, you'll build more authority and earn reciprocity when you comment 10 times for every one post you publish.

Take Emily, a regional account executive who'd always treated LinkedIn like a digital résumé. She rarely posted, never commented, and assumed her network wasn't paying attention anyway.

That changed after she lost a deal to a competitor who was everywhere on LinkedIn—engaging, commenting, and showing up in her buyers' feeds.

Emily committed to the 10:1 method. Each morning, over coffee, she scrolled through her feed with purpose. She liked, commented, shared, and tagged others thoughtfully. Emily didn't overthink it—she just started showing up.

Within a month, her visibility had exploded. Her name kept appearing in the right conversations. One of her prospects commented on a post she had replied to and sent her a message: "Hey, I keep seeing you pop up. We should talk."

That conversation turned into a meeting. The meeting turned into a proposal. And within 45 days, Emily had closed one of her biggest deals of the year.

Avoid the Post and Ghost

Far too many salespeople drop a great post into the stream that pulls in comments but fail to acknowledge that engagement.

Rather than responding to those comments and participating in a dialogue with their followers, they ghost them.

When someone comments on your post, it's personal. They're acknowledging the value you provided and opening the door to a conversation. When you post and ghost, it's like turning your back to someone at a networking event who is holding their hand out to shake yours.

LinkedIn isn't a broadcast platform—it's a conversation forum. Failing to acknowledge the comments on your posts is not only rude behavior, it's a wasted opportunity.

The fix is simple. Monitor every post. When you get comments, respond—even if it's a simple "thank you for your insight." With particularly thoughtful comments, ask follow-up questions to start a conversation. The LinkedIn algorithm rewards it, but more importantly, so does your audience.

Showing Up Is a Daily Discipline

You don't need hours each day to show up on LinkedIn. All you need is a locked-in daily routine. Before you post, comment on five posts in your feed. After you post, comment on five more, then check back on your original post and respond to comments there.

You can be even more purposeful when you use LinkedIn's filters—free and Sales Navigator—to find specific content to comment on that aligns with your personal branding, prospecting, and sales objectives.

Focus your attention where it counts: the right people, the right topics, the right timing. Leveraging the filter techniques you learned in Part 1, search by:

- Keywords or topics in your industry
- People: prospects, thought leaders, clients, or peers

- Post type: videos, articles, live sessions, or company news
- "Top" or "Latest" search strings to sort by relevance or recency

Seek out the conversations you want to be part of, and prioritize posts that already have some engagement—they're more likely to give you visibility and lead to conversations.

Comments with Substance

When you comment on a post, don't just say, "Great point" or "Love this." Say why and comment with substance:

- Share an experience that connects.
- Offer a different angle.
- When appropriate, ask a thoughtful question to prompt dialogue.
- Add a unique perspective that brings value to the conversation.
- Aim for clarity and brevity in your posts. Overly lengthy comments can overwhelm readers.
- Foster a constructive and collaborative environment. Adopt the "Yes, and . . ." technique to build upon others' ideas, rather than contradicting them directly.
- Proofread your comments to avoid typographical and grammatical errors that reflect poorly on your personal brand.
- When someone engages with you, acknowledge it, publicly and thoughtfully.

As you comment, tag others (@mention) for whom the content will be relevant, to bring them into the conversation.

The LinkedIn Edge All Comes Down to Showing Up

Want more engagement, more leads, a larger network, more followers, less resistance from prospects, and more sales conversations? Then show up on LinkedIn.

When you make showing up a habit, you will become a trusted voice in your niche. You'll cross your prospects' familiarity threshold. You will gain authority, build your pipeline, and become a lead magnet.

You will win more, earn more, and sell more, because you will have gained *The LinkedIn Edge*.

About the Authors

Jeb Blount and **Brynne Tillman** came together to write *The LinkedIn Edge* with a shared mission: to help sales professionals master the art and science of building modern pipelines.

Jeb, author of *Fanatical Prospecting*, brings decades of expertise in high-velocity outbound prospecting, sales discipline, and pipeline management.

Brynne, one of the world's foremost LinkedIn and digital sales experts, brings unmatched knowledge of trust-based social engagement and relationship-first selling.

Together, they deliver a proven system for integrating LinkedIn, AI, and outbound prospecting strategy to drive more conversations, create more opportunities, and close more deals.

Readers can go even deeper with both authors through courses on Sales Gravy University. There, Jeb and Brynne each teach lessons that expand on the ideas in this book—from prospecting mastery and sequence design to LinkedIn strategy, AI driven sales tactics, and digital-first sales motions. If you're ready to build a bigger, better, more qualified pipeline—both online and offline—there's no better place to start than Sales Gravy University.

Both authors share a simple belief: Technology may change, but sales is still a human-to-human game.

Jeb Blount is the author or co-author of 18 of the most definitive books ever written on sales and sales leadership. He is an in-demand keynote speaker and is among the world's most respected thought leaders on sales, AI, leadership, and customer experience.

Through his global training and consulting organization, Sales Gravy, Jeb and his team train, advise, build playbooks for, and provide fractional sales leadership for a who's who of the world's most prestigious organizations.

His sales training platform, Sales Gravy University, is used by more than 70,000 companies and sales professionals to hone skills and gain a winning edge.

Jeb's popular podcast Sales Gravy is the #1 ranked sales specific podcast worldwide and his website SalesGravy.com includes thousands of articles and free sales training resources to help sales professionals, entrepreneurs, and leaders sell more.

Connect with Jeb on LinkedIn, X, Facebook, YouTube, TikTok, and Instagram. Listen to his *Sales Gravy* podcast on Apple, iHeart, or Spotify.

To schedule Jeb to speak at your next event, call 1-888-360-2249, email brooke@salesgravy.com or carrie@salesgravy.com, or visit www.jebblount.com. You may email Jeb directly at jeb@salesgravy.com.

 **Brynne Tillman** is a recognized LinkedIn and AI for Sales trainer and Official LinkedIn Insider who empowers sales professionals to elevate their social selling and prompt writing skills.

As the driving force behind *Social Sales Link* and askSSL.ai, she champions authentic relationship-building, helping revenue-generating professionals start more trust-based conversations without being salesy.

Brynne is also the co-author of *Prompt Writing Made Easy* with Generations Inked Publishing.

Index